CBT Workbook for Adult Mental Health

How to Stop Negative Thinking, Relieve Anxiety, Worry Less, and Start Living

PUBLISHED BY: Stanley Sheppard

© Copyright _____ 2023 - **All rights reserved.**

The content contained within this book may not be reproduced, duplicated or transmitted without direct written permission from the author or the publisher.

Under no circumstances will any blame or legal responsibility be held against the publisher, or author, for any damages, reparation, or monetary loss due to the information contained within this book. Either directly or indirectly. You are responsible for your own choices, actions, and results.

Legal Notice:
This book is copyright protected. This book is only for personal use. You cannot amend, distribute, sell, use, quote or paraphrase any part, or the content within this book, without the consent of the author or publisher.

Disclaimer Notice:
Please note the information contained within this document is for educational and entertainment purposes only. All effort has been executed to present accurate, up to date, and reliable, complete information. No warranties of any kind are declared or implied. Readers acknowledge that the author is not engaging in the rendering of legal, financial, medical or professional advice.

By reading this document, the reader agrees that under no circumstances is the author responsible for any losses, direct or indirect, which are incurred as a result of the use of the information contained within this document, including, but not limited to, — errors, omissions, or inaccuracies.

Complimentary CBT Journal

To get access just go to the webpage or scan QR code:
https://greatlifebooks.com/CBT-Journal

Enhance your journey towards cognitive-behavioral transformation with the CBT Journal, thoughtfully designed to complement and enrich your experience with the CBT Workbook. This journal is your personalized space to delve deeper into your thoughts, emotions, and progress as you engage in the transformative exercises outlined in the workbook.

With pages designed to encourage self-reflection, goal-setting, and tracking your CBT practices, this journal is the perfect tool to amplify the benefits of cognitive-behavioral therapy. Take your commitment to self-improvement to the next level and unlock the full potential of cognitive-behavioral transformation with this insightful and complementary journal.

Table of Contents

Introduction 1

A Deep Dive into CBT 7

Where to Begin 28

Common Cognitive Distortions 53

Understanding Anxiety and Depression 75

CBT Techniques for Anxiety and
Depression 101

CBT for Stress Management 135

Winding Up 171

Thank You 179

References 180

Your Free Bonus

As a way of saying thanks for your purchase, I'm offering these FOUR books for **FREE** to my readers. To get access just go to: https://greatlifebooks.com/CBT-Workbook-free-bonus

- ❖ **CBT for Procrastination Workbook**: How to overcome procrastination, boost productivity, and take control of your life
- ❖ **8 Highly Effective Ways to Relieve Stress**: The ultimate guide to stress management
- ❖ **Overcome Anxiety**: How to stop the cycle of anxiety, worry and fear so you can regain control of your life
- ❖ **Resilience**: How to build mental strength to overcome any difficult situation and live a better life

Don't let stress control your life any longer. Take charge and discover the secrets to a calmer, more enjoyable existence. Download these free books now and start your transformation today!

Introduction

Awareness is the greatest agent for change.

- Eckhart Tolle (2005)

Is man capable of change?

My father is a bitter man. All my life, I have known him to come home often drunk and in one of two states- deliriously happy and easy or angry and blaming everyone for everything. The latter was more common, and I suffered anxiety each evening, wondering in what state the man would come and whether I would receive the third earful of the week.

Though I was too young to understand Freud's concepts and the workings of the mind, it felt as though he struggled with something. As though he wasn't a horrible person, perhaps he just... felt dark and twisted inside. And that darkness caused him to say and do horrible things.

Yet this darkness was not ever-present. There were days he showered his family with love. When he celebrated the food his wife placed at the table and his children's laughter around him. It was almost easy to forget the other person until he flipped the table in disgust at the same plate of rice he praised last week.

It was almost intriguing to see how similar events prompted such different reactions. One day he would play with our family cat but kicked her out the next because 'feeding her was an expensive affair. 'Today he liked a compliment on his jacket but would hate a similar comment two weeks later. There seemed to lay something beyond the words and the actions. Something that guided how he reacted but which was lost on us.

In trying to understand the man, I first encountered Beck and cognitive-behavioral therapy.

CBT holds that there is a significant link between our thoughts, emotions, and behavior, and though I could not see inside his head, it finally felt like a piece fell into place.

Cognitive-behavioral therapy (CBT) has shown remarkable strength in managing numerous mental health disorders like depression, anxiety, and OCD, eating disorders, sleep disorders, among others (Nakao et al., 2021). Moreover, the tools have proven effective in addressing the most ordinary, everyday challenges- the worry we cannot help. The fears we secretly carry. The weight of negative thinking that quietly keeps us under a dark cloud, even on a hot summer's day.

It has been decades since I was the boy afraid of his father's outbursts. Determined to help people have a more positive outlook on life, I immersed myself in teaching. Over time, conversations with my students and colleagues ranged across career goals and expectations, life-work-study balance, self-awareness and personal growth, relationships, and so much more.

The conversations often ran deep, sometimes arriving at the confession that life can be overwhelming. Family and loved ones are a source of deep love and acceptance, yet they often cause immense distress. Work gives us a sense of meaning and drive, yet its demands can and have attempted to drive many crazy. We want to offer ourselves the best, yet we cannot always spare ourselves from the worst.

We all struggle with the hardships of being a human being that exists with ourselves and others. And even the most optimistic person has trouble smiling sometimes.

Yet we must live. We must thrive. So how do we achieve that in a world that is not always sunshine and rainbows? How do we remain motivated and self-assured through the seemingly effortless and hard days?

Well, awareness, as Tolle emphasized, is a great place to start. But awareness alone is insufficient. And this is what I found compelling about CBT.

In an era that relies heavily on solutions backed by scientific study and empirical evidence, CBT presents the idea that we can actively participate in unearthing unproductive thoughts and patterns and designing practical problem-solving tools.

And herein lays the first nugget: We hold the capacity to effect the change we want. We can be part of the work, and no solution lies outside of ourselves or beyond our reach.

This is what this workbook is about, really.

Think of it as an instrument that first brings you to the awareness of your thoughts and the emotions and behaviors causing and resulting from them. In the book, we shall delve into the development of CBT as an effective psychotherapy treatment option. We shall look at the thought patterns and disorders that CBT is effective with. We shall turn our insight into action with simple exercises that help reframe negative thoughts into a more positive and balanced state.

Is this book for everyone? That depends on how you look at it.

CBT is often recommended for disorders like anxiety and depression. But every human on earth encounters negative thoughts which may trigger unhelpful reactions. Every human could benefit from learning to arrest their not-so-great thoughts and turn them into good energy sources.

As a child, I often thought, "I'm not a good enough child for my parents, and that is why Dad shouts at me." "I do everything wrong." "I am not loved. "Various CBT tools finally helped me realize that these thoughts diminished my quality of life and that I was not responsible for what others (my father) chose to say and do. The only thing I was responsible for were my thoughts and actions, and I could reframe some of these thoughts to, "I will sometimes make mistakes, but that does not make me a bad person or child."

Of course, I must emphasize that this is not a book of spells that will magically treat whatever ails you. Nor is it a shortcut to avoiding the actual work because the truth is, working on yourself is a true labor of love.

And this is the second nugget: Even with all the support in the world, the buck still stops with you. You are your own Superman. You have to get down and dirty, and isn't that exciting?

The CBT Workbook Checklist

So, what do you need to experience this book successfully? Place a mark against these items as you gauge your readiness to take on the 'you' challenge:

Item	Purpose	Check
1. An open mind	Change begins with the willingness to look at things differently.	☐
2. A healthy amount of skepticism	We all have what works and what doesn't. Not every tool may necessarily work for you.	☐
3. Grace	The journey may be treacherous, and facing yourself and your genuine thoughts and beliefs is not always delightful. Yet you have to regard yourself with compassion as you would someone under your care.	☐
4. Patience	Change takes time. Allow it.	☐
5. Consistency	We have to keep at the work consistently for there to be tangible progress. Don't quit, especially when you want to the most. After all, it is always darkest before dawn.	☐

Most of all, I invite you to consider that the circumstances that led to you opening this book in the first place are not a bad thing. Everything we go through is part of our life experience. Therefore, every pain point is an opportunity for growth and greater self-awareness. It allows us to see the world from a more knowledgeable perspective and develop new skills. And just as a diamond is refined through fire, we are made authentic the more we see and challenge our pre-conditionings in search of our truest and highest selves.

Important disclaimer:

This workbook is not intended for diagnosing, preventing, or treating any disorder, nor a substitute for a healthcare provider's assessment and advice. Seek professional counsel if you struggle with a medical or mental health challenge.

Let us dive into it, shall we?

A Deep Dive into CBT

You have two choices, to control your mind or to let your mind control you.

-Paulo Coelho (2006)

We must first appreciate how it works to understand why cognitive-behavioral therapy is immensely acclaimed. In this chapter, we shall delve into therapy through the ages up to the birth of CBT and its various applications. We shall look at the multiple disorders that CBT demonstrates effectiveness in managing and the principles that strengthen the therapy.

By the end of this chapter, you should have a clearer picture of CBT and its usefulness in daily life.

A seemingly mundane event happened in my class a while back that I thought may help paint a picture as we go along:

> I taught Communication and Management courses at a local college for about five years. I liked to give each class random, voluntary assessments every few weeks for two reasons.
>
> First, they took their compulsory exam at the end of the semester, and these tests were great practice. Second, the random assessments helped me gauge students' understanding of the course material. With standard, scheduled quizzes and midterms,

pulling an all-nighter cramming session was easy just before the exam. I remember doing this when I was in university and missing out on so much knowledge because I needed to take the time to understand. The random assessments thus painted a more accurate picture of how my class was fairing and what we needed to revisit.

This Thursday morning, I came to class with the marked quizzes and got into a discussion of their performance. The questions had been deliberately challenging, and I wanted to test their application capacity.

Julian, the class clown, laughed at his dismal score and quickly put the paper away. He did this each time and thus far had not bothered with the prompts to study harder and improve.

Katrina was always one of the best-performing students, but she wore a troubled face as she looked at her paper. This paper had been tough, and she had scored considerably poorer than previous tests. She was the third best this time. Katrina was silent for most of the rest of the class.

Simon smiled as he muttered, 'Looks like the studying is paying off.' He had scored the highest points for the first time all semester and was pleasantly surprised.

Perhaps the only one who seemed more troubled than Katrina was Paul, who said nothing, just as he had said nothing when he got the lowest score on the last test. He asked to be excused from the class and returned the next, considerably more at ease. He missed the following quiz.

In the above illustration, my students reacted diversely to their seemingly similar results. While Katrina and Simon had done well, the former was disappointed while the latter celebrated. Similarly, Julian and Paul were at the bottom of the rank, yet Julian was unaffected, but Paul left the class and missed the following quiz.

How could one event elicit such different reactions?

French philosopher Rene Descartes offered that except your own thought, there is nothing in your power (Descartes, 2008). These words echo those of other great men and women that understood the power of thinking to create or to destroy. Roman emperor and philosopher Marcus Aurelius remarked that the happiness of one's life depends upon the quality of their thoughts (n.d.), suggesting that while life events may be uncontrollable, we have the power to choose our quality of life regardless.

These sentiments point to the idea that while human beings react to situations, which is normal, perhaps it is not the events that prompt our specific reaction but our interpretation of these events. It may not be getting a flat tire and getting late to work that causes us to be in a bad mood all day, but how we interpret that inconvenient event. Perhaps it is not failing a test that makes us feel miserable but how we interpret that failure.

This same belief in the power of our thoughts to impact our mood and actions presented itself in the world of psychology more than a century ago when Freud observed that talking about their painful life history helped patients with hysteria relieve pent-up emotion (Kenny, 2016).

Freud and the Advent of Psychoanalysis

Freud proposed that the human mind is made of the conscious component, where current thoughts and feelings exist, and the larger preconscious and unconscious mind, which holds processes that steer our primitive and instinctive behavior. His studies supposed that sexual desires in childhood were repressed from the conscious mind yet were some of the most potent unconscious thought processes. These propositions and his research into the constant internal conflict between the instinctual drives and the conscience formed the basis for psychoanalysis even today.

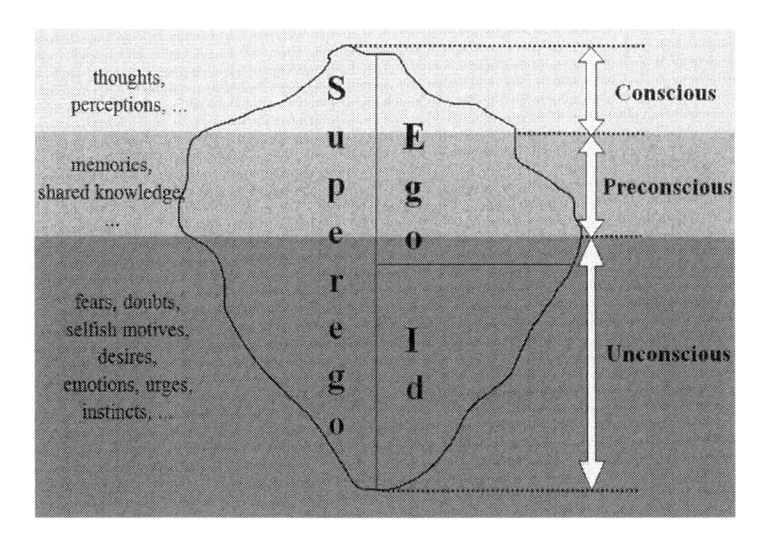

The Freudian model of the human mind takes the shape of an iceberg as below (The 'Iceberg Metaphor'-Freud's Vision of the Mind [54]- Scientific Diagram, n.d.):

His migration into the US ballooned experimental and applied psychology and psychoanalysis as a tool for relieving client discomfort held until the 1960s and '70s.

Suppose Paul had visited a psychoanalyst during this period, concerned about walking out of class after failing a test. In that case, the therapist might have guided him into a conversation about his childhood and upbringing. Did his father reprimand him often that he silently associated every setback with total failure? Was he punished at school for failing tests and developed fear and anxiety about examinations?

Paul may have spent an indefinite time visiting his therapist, interpreting his unconscious conflicts and their motivations.

They may have analyzed the repetitions he exhibited presently as a result of the conflicts from his past.

By the 1950s, however, criticism about the capacity of psychoanalysis to respond to shifting social needs after the Second World War coincided with the evolution of behavioral therapy.

Behavioral Therapy

The work of behavioral scientists like Pavlov found that conditioning in animals is automatic and, therefore, behavior can be taught. Indeed, Mittens, our family cat for many years, always knew to come running into the kitchen whenever she heard the sound of the opening fridge door. She knew that was where we kept her food, and we often fed her while we got food for ourselves. While not every time the fridge door was open meant dinnertime in the perfect Pavlovian bell-means-food set-up, she was undoubtedly correct two times a day.

Additional studies into behaviorism examined how behavior is taught, leading to the learning models in use today: Reinforce a positive habit by reward. Punish a negative habit to discourage it.

These models were the foundation for behavioral therapy. This short-term treatment relieved distress by increasing the exposure to the triggering event or minimizing the associated effect the trigger caused. Both strategies aimed to ultimately alter the unhelpful behavior by eliminating its need.

Here, the therapist would probably focus on Paul skipping the following quiz, and how to stop it. He may suggest taking more tests to get used to the energy around examinations and results. Alternatively, he may propose that Paul take up extra sessions or group work to improve his grasp of the subject matter and consequently perform better, thereby eliminating the need to 'escape' from class.

Although animal conditioning models formed the basis for a look into human behaviorism, they overlooked human thinking processes and their impact. In a few decades, behavioral therapy had evolved.

Cognitive Therapy

The cognitive revolution of the 60s stressed that personal verbal and cognitive abilities influenced human conditioning, and psychotherapy took a giant leap forward. The new behavioral models abandoned associative learning to consider the role of thoughts and feelings in setting human behavior. They proposed that a critical component needed to be added to previous models, birthing cognitive therapy.

Cognitive therapy provides a key component in human behavior: It is essential to understand how a person perceives an event to comprehend why they act the way they do. To understand how a person feels, we must understand their thoughts.

For instance, if the flat tire incident happened to Cole, it could be visualized as:

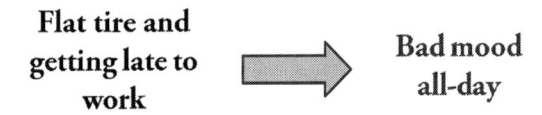

Flat tire and getting late to work ⟹ **Bad mood all-day**

Say that this same event happened to Greg, but he showed up to work happy as a clam and possibly talking about his macho self to the ladies in the breakroom.

What made Cole different?

The answer is the missing component- How Cole perceived the event and what it meant. It is the thoughts about the event that fuel the emotional response.

Perhaps this is what happened to Cole as he changed the tire:

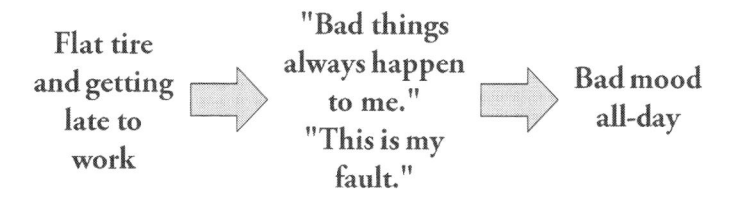

| Flat tire and getting late to work | ⟹ | "Bad things always happen to me." "This is my fault." | ⟹ | Bad mood all-day |

A psychotherapist in this era would have poked at the thoughts and emotions occurring to my student, Paul, at getting his paper. Paul may have admitted to feeling like a loser and thinking that surely he must not be good at anything. He may have learned that Paul got anxious before tests and struggled to relax through them.

His process may have looked something like this:

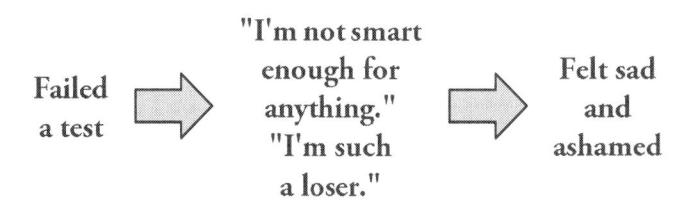

| Failed a test | ⟹ | "I'm not smart enough for anything." "I'm such a loser." | ⟹ | Felt sad and ashamed |

The therapist may have suggested that his mind perhaps associated failing the test with more than limited course understanding. He may have then asked Paul to create a list of things he was good at and those he wasn't, allowing the idea that one cannot be good at everything, but that does not mean that *they aren't good at anything*. Therefore, he did not have to associate failing a quiz with 'being a loser.' He may have asked Paul to allow himself to take more tests, even independently, to get used to them and find that they were not as nerve-wracking.

As therapy models shifted to place cognitive awareness at the center while maintaining an objective perspective, cognitive and behavioral therapy merged, and CBT was born.

Cognitive Behavioral Therapy - An Integrated Approach

We can trace CBT's baby steps to the work of Albert Ellis and Aaron Beck. While conducting experiments on psychoanalytic concepts, Beck found that patients with depression experienced involuntary flows of negative thoughts, which seemed to center on three subjects- themselves, the world, and the future (Beck et al., 1979).

A patient would, for instance, express:

> *"There is something wrong with me/ I cannot get anything right/ I am inadequate."*
>
> *"I do not belong anywhere."*
>
> *"Everything is pointless."*

He believed these thoughts resulted from maladaptive processes formed during childhood, which became the bedrock for what he coined 'automatic negative thoughts.'

Meanwhile, Ellis' study of irrational thoughts found that irrational belief systems formed the link between negative feelings and behavior that resulted from an 'activating event' (David et al., 2009).

Fundamentally, CBT proposes interconnectedness between thoughts, beliefs, emotions, and behavior, each affecting the other and rising from a triggering situation.

For example, when a person afraid of rollercoasters *feels* uneasy about getting on a ride, they will likely *think* how dangerous it is and want to opt out.

Likewise, if the same person *thinks* that a rollercoaster is unsafe, they are likely to *be* afraid to get on and want to sit it out.

The interrelatedness of thoughts, feelings, and behavior is illustrated below:

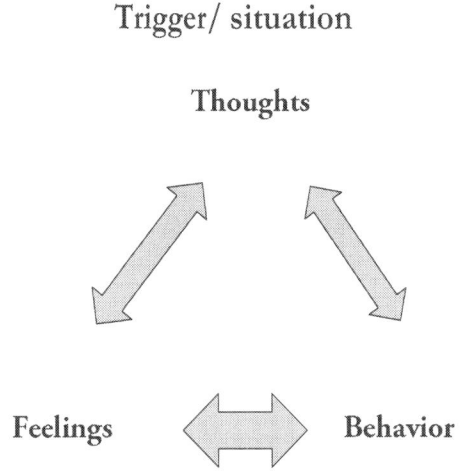

Trigger/ situation

Thoughts

Feelings ⟷ **Behavior**

Having understood this relationship, Paul could complete the diagram below and see how his thoughts about his performance affected his mood and caused him to 'escape.' He would see that the more they festered, the more they culminated in unhelpful behavior like skipping class and tests:

Trigger/ situation
Failing a test

Thoughts:

'I am a failure.'
'I do not belong in this class.'
'I will probably fail this class.'

Feelings:

Sad. Defeated. Ashamed.

Behavior:

Walking out of class. Missing the following quiz.

This awareness, however, is not meant to diminish or invalidate our thoughts and emotions. Using the illustration of fearing rollercoasters: The engineering work to build one is hardly fool-proof, and there have been defective rides. It makes sense to be afraid and think that you are unsafe. CBT examines to what extent these thoughts cause unhelpful patterns and the distortions that need rewiring. Is the fear so intense that you miss out on fun family or friend experiences you would have wanted to be part of? Are there alarming effects while on a ride, like panic attacks?

In this case, a CBT therapist introduces skepticism into the cognitive cycle. They recommend activities like going on the internet and finding actual statistics on rollercoaster safety to compare thought versus evidence. They may suggest starting with simpler rides to work into the realization that while immensely thrilling, the rides are not dangerous.

CBT Today

CBT models continue to evolve with new techniques like Acceptance and Commitment Therapy borrowing the CBT tools but directing them toward a different goal. The therapy varies by not teaching people to change their thoughts about a triggering event. Instead, they focus on liberating the person from the event itself by accepting and allowing the feelings about the occasion.

Activity

Review the random activities that happened recently, a day or week ago, or within the past month. Consider an event you felt strongly about, perhaps fear, anger, or sadness.

Describe the details you remember about the event in the field provided. In the other spaces, write down how you remember feeling, the thoughts that came to mind, and what you did.

Write down as many as you can recall, as honestly as possible.

Event	How I felt:

What I thought:	What I did:

Were there any correlations between your thoughts, feelings, and actions? Could you indicate them using arrows?

It is okay if the correlation does not occur to you immediately. Because so many thoughts and emotions are automatic, they may not be noticeable initially. We will revisit this CBT cycle often in the book, working to unearth this connectedness as it manifests in different people and situations. By the end of the workbook, you should easily map out these patterns in random, day-to-day, distressing events and understand your automatic thoughts and emotions more easily.

Now, let us focus on the disorders that CBT is impactful for and the principles and misconceptions underlying the therapy techniques.

Disorders that CBT Helps Manage

Research indicates that CBT exhibits observable progress in managing these conditions (Nakao et al., 2021b):

- Anger and aggression
- Anxiety disorders

- Bipolar disorder
- Chronic pain and fatigue
- Criminal behavior
- Eating disorders
- Depression and dysthymia
- Distress due to a medical condition
- Distress due to pregnancy complications
- General stress
- Insomnia
- Schizophrenia and other psychotic disorders
- Sleep disorders
- Somatic symptom disorders
- Substance use disorder

The Principles of CBT

1. CBT is goal-oriented

As we have covered above, CBT anchors heavily on the idea that our thoughts influence how we feel about a situation and how we behave.

Therefore, the purpose for engaging in this kind of therapy should be precise- You are not walking in to tinker around and see what you can dig up. Instead, the goal must be clear from the get-go, and the tools targeted at achieving the desired change. Progress will be easier to measure, and you can tell what is effective and what needs tweaking.

2. CBT requires collaboration

Teamwork is vital to the success of CBT. When we think of treating an ailment, we know that options like pills and injections work one way- we take them in, and they do their job. Surgery would remove growth in the body: You lie on the table, perhaps unconscious, while the doctor gets to work. There is the professional or the tool. We are the patient.

Treating the inner person is different. It is a process that involves two specialists: The therapist brings in their knowledge and expertise in cognitive behavioral therapy while you supply the knowledge and expertise about your being.

Collaboration is possible even while self-practicing without a therapist. This workbook provides the knowledge of CBT and needs to combine with self-awareness for progress.

3. CBT is structured

When talking to a friend about your challenges, it is easy to get lost in the details and spiral into other subjects. I laugh when I consider how my friends and I catch up: We don't see each other often, and when we do, 20 tabs are open within half an hour. A 'tab' is how we refer to our stories, and the fun part is trying to find where we started hours later.

While talking to a friend is always helpful, lacking targeted focus could hinder internal conflict resolution.

CBT demands structure. Treatment follows a system that builds upon itself, starting with setting clear goals and then laying out how to get there. Preceding sessions lay the foundation for the next. For instance, Chapter 3 will delve into the cognitive distortions that reinforce negative thoughts and emotions, and the following chapters will focus on changing these thoughts and, ultimately, our behavior.

4. CBT is time-bound

The average CBT program with a therapist is ten to 20 one-hour-long sessions. The tools are designed to be effective within the shortest time possible. Clear goals and a good structure will help achieve the time constraint, making CBT affordable and fast.

5. CBT is present-focused

CBT focuses on current events, seeking to change our present thoughts. This is not to mean that the therapy invalidates the impact of past experiences and socialization on our mental form. Instead, while these past experiences form our beliefs and affect how we react to present situations, the tools focus on changing negative thoughts and behavior for current resolution.

6. CBT is evidence-based

Numerous research studies on CBT effectiveness indicate remarkable transformative progress. Therapists rely on these tested techniques as they are measurable and help define variables like the treatment duration.

Moreover, each session provides for data collection and analysis, with you and the therapist using the information you supply to diagnose the underlying distortions and their intensity and therefore design workable recommendations.

Working with a self-help workbook like this means you are your data source and analyst, with the various exercises helping you draw correlations and solutions.

7. CBT is proactive

If you can't take the heat, stay out of the kitchen. Like the advice to take our lives by the metaphorical horns, CBT requires conscious and intentional engagement.

Only work produces change, and somebody must get down and dirty. You must be committed to your goals and to the work it takes. Think of yourself (and your therapist) as the workers that built Rome, brick by brick, for all the days the great empire demanded.

8. CBT is practice-oriented

Changing my thought patterns is a lot like when I started running. At first, I couldn't do more than a few hundred steps before my heart started calling 911. However, the more I showed up on the track, the stronger I got and ran further. Now I prepare for annual marathons and stay strong by the finish line.

Likewise, CBT tools require practice for tangible progress. For example, filling in a journal with your daily thoughts will make evaluating how they have changed over the month much more meaningful than once-a-week entries.

9. CBT teaches skills

Whether working with a therapist or by yourself, the goal of CBT is simple: To help identify negative thought patterns and change them for positive emotions and behavior.

The tools herein equip you with the skills to manage your challenges even past the treatment period. They are a valuable lifestyle change even years after the first walk down this road.

The Misconceptions about CBT

CBT is not immune to misconceptions about how it works and its effectiveness. In this section, we shall quickly consider what we may have heard about CBT, which is off the mark.

1. CBT focuses on the mind, not our feelings

There is much talk of thoughts, changing negative distortions, and so forth in CBT, which may suggest that our feelings are unimportant in treatment. On the contrary, our feelings often make us aware that something is off.

If you are afraid of heights but find yourself at the top of a building, the natural reactions may include an accelerated heartbeat, sweaty palms, and dizziness. If you went to a therapist, you might begin by saying, 'I was up there and paralyzed with fear. I was so scared. I thought I was going to fall to my death.'

Our emotions are valid and necessary pointers in the CBT process. While our thoughts may trigger emotions, we are often more aware of how we feel than what we think. In this illustration, you and the therapist will likely use how you feel about heights to see the thoughts relating to this trigger and, therefore, the behavior.

2. CBT is positive thinking

Some people believe that thinking positively will automatically lead to feeling positive. While CBT focuses on altering negative thoughts and, therefore, can be said to be the motivational speaker of therapy, it is more than a simple flip of the coin.

It would not be enough to tell Katrina that she will do well in her following quiz and should not feel bad about not getting the results she wants now. CBT explores the distortions about her feeling like a failure, prompting her to evaluate how exaggerated they are and form a more encouraging frame of mind toward her studies and exams.

3. CBT has no regard for past experiences

As reiterated in the principles of CBT, the tools focus on present situations and changing current thoughts to a more positive outlook. However, this does not mean that there is no focus on past experiences and our core beliefs. Instead, CBT aims to resolve a person's present distress by evaluating the current thoughts that may be driving this emotional unrest rather than fault past situations which cannot be undone.

While growing up with my father contributed to my feelings of self-doubt and self-loathing, CBT would focus on my current environment to address debilitating self-criticism- my work, my family, that trip to the store where someone called me old, and how these circumstances reinforce the negative distortions, rather than what the man said to me when I was nine.

4. CBT works only for intelligent or expressive people

CBT involves many activities that may appear complex at the onset. A patient is expected to divulge extensive personal information. They need to be aware of their distortions and their emotional effects. They must apply realistic reasoning to challenge these distortions and design more helpful thought patterns.

While all this sounds daunting, practical CBT tools are simple, so they take seemingly complex concepts and work them into easy-to-chew-and-swallow activities and sessions.

How Helpful is CBT?

Intricate fields like medicine rely on accurate and reliable research for effective progress. These scientific inquiries have evolved to incorporate meta-analyses performed where numerous studies are targeted at the same questions, each bearing results with a margin for error. Meta-analyses combine statistics from these studies to derive a general truth with less room for error and are reliable measures for evidence-based techniques like CBT.

A survey considered a sample of 106 out of 269 meta-analytic studies for CBT application in various disorders (Hofmann et al., 2012). The survey found that CBT had more significant support for managing anxiety disorders, somatoform disorders, bulimia, anger control problems, and general stress. Moreover, studies comparing the CBT response rate and other treatments or controls found that CBT exhibited higher response rates than comparing treatments.

Another study found that CBT holds a higher standard compared to other psychotherapies because there is enormous research in this form of psychotherapy. Moreover, CBT models align with the current age's mind and behavior patterns, including data processing (David et al., 2018).

What makes CBT such a powerful tool?

Techniques like breathwork have existed for millennia across the world. The Orient has kept to traditional rituals like meditation which it shares with the contemporary Western world for wellness and balance. While relatively new in practice, CBT aligns these tools with the timeless principle that our thoughts shape us, but we have the power to shape these thoughts.

CBT is so impactful because it directs our effort to a particular point, allowing us to wade into the work of undoing helpful patterns without being overwhelmed by the pressure to do everything at once.

These tools emphasize practice to be effective. This way, you reinforce what you are learning each day through action. Additionally, CBT breaks the cycle of unhelpful thoughts that run amok when we are emotionally distressed. Consistent practice improves our capacity to break out of this hellish loop, and we find that the more we catch ourselves and rewire our thoughts, the easier and faster it becomes.

Finally, CBT is skill oriented, so we are equipped to deal with challenges even post-treatment. By the end of this workbook, the goal is to be more aware of your thoughts and better at arresting and reworking what is unhelpful for the rest of your life.

In this chapter, we have gone over the evolution of CBT, the disorders it helps manage, its principles and misconceptions, and what makes it impactful. In the following chapters, we will get into the first steps in CBT, tools to help undo negative thoughts, and the techniques for disorders like anxiety, depression, stress, and procrastination.

Where to Begin

No great thing is created suddenly.

- Epictetus (1865)

In the previous chapter, we looked into the evolution of psychoanalysis and psychotherapy and the advent of cognitive-behavioral therapy. We considered how thoughts affect our emotions and subsequent behavior, the loop binding these three elements, and how CBT helps to undo negative thought patterns. Finally, we identified the principles of CBT and what makes it an effective treatment for numerous disorders like anxiety and depression.

In this chapter, we shall prepare for the next part of the workbook. We shall delve into getting ready for a CBT program and the therapy steps. We shall also discuss practicing CBT on your own with the help of tools like this workbook and how to stay motivated while on the course.

First, let us revisit the overarching intentions of CBT.

Cognitive behavioral therapy is unlike traditional talk therapy because it is structured and highly goal-oriented. The treatment aims to help a person identify and address maladaptive thought patterns, underlying beliefs, and behavior that may be causing discomfort.

First, **CBT fosters the monitoring of our cognitive processes**. Research conducted by a team at Queen's University, Kingston, indicates that the average mind has about 6,000 thoughts per day, termed 'thought worms' (Tseng & Poppenk, 2020). This implies that we have approximately 250 thoughts every hour and four thoughts every minute. At the most basic level, we have a new thought worm every 15 seconds.

While our thoughts are as random as *how far the Simpsons' seasons are now* up to *the fish species found in Fiji,* some thought patterns tend to be repetitive. When distressed, these repetitive thoughts lean toward the negative anchored on our cemented core beliefs. In the next chapter, we shall delve into these thought patterns, identified by Aaron Beck as 'automatic negative thoughts.'

With the practical techniques in CBT, such as journaling, we become more aware of the thoughts running amok and can identify negative ones faster. This way, we can arrest them before they have done their damage. These techniques also help to read emotions, and we can question feelings like frustration and inadequacy to uncover the automatic thoughts prompting them. CBT helps to realize how our distorted thought patterns lead to the painful feelings we experience and therefore appreciate the ability to see them as they come and go.

Next, **CBT establishes positive problem-solving skills**. Again, we tend to fall into escapist patterns when we suffer distress. A person with social anxiety will tend to avoid social situations, even if that is unhelpful and perhaps detrimental to their life and status. People under stress may fall into addictive devices such as drugs and alcohol, possibly damaging their productivity and relationships.

CBT introduces alternative methods to solve current problems and quickly reduce suffering. For example, gradual exposure to situations that trigger anxiety helps unearth the truth- people are not so scary and hardly think about us as furiously as we imagine. Factual evidence shows how dangerous things like heights, dogs, and elevators are, justifying or contradicting the need for our reactions.

Finally, **CBT tools help patients return to a productive daily routine**. As we shall see in the chapter on depression, mental and emotional unrest can cause detrimental effects like disrupted sleep and feeding patterns, immense fatigue, and challenges concentrating on tasks. These problems will likely affect our productive capacity, making it harder to meet work obligations, cater to our families, participate in social activities, etc.

CBT aims to prevent future episodes of distress, allowing a steady return to wellness. When you have succeeded in arresting unhelpful thoughts, interrogating them, and judging them as invalid, you can reframe how you look at yourself and the world. Moreover, these tools nurture a sense of control over self and external forces, reinforcing the awareness that your life is in your hands, as is the ability and capacity to make it what you desire.

CBT Step-by-Step

A typical CBT program follows a step-by-step plan, with each step feeding into the next and every previous step providing a stepping stone for the present.

1. Identifying negative thoughts and habits

As elaborated above, CBT works by identifying and undoing unhelpful thoughts, beliefs, and emotions. Identifying negative patterns is the first step, and it must be brutally honest.

When trying to effect change, you must ask, 'Where am I now?' to idealize the length of the road ahead. In this phase, the techniques aim to draw attention to the thoughts occurring in the motions of distress, bringing them to the surface and recording them for deeper analysis.

Tools that help with this phase include a daily journal indicating any triggering events and how you felt, thought, and acted on them. Additionally, lists help to dig up all the many variations of the negative thoughts, providing insight into the breadth of the distortions and the resulting actions.

For example, breaking up with a partner could prompt as many thoughts as-

> *"I'm not pretty or interesting. No wonder they left me."*
>
> *"I'm such a loser."*
>
> *"No one could love a mess like me."*
>
> *"Maybe if I lost weight, they would still love me."*
>
> *"I bet they left me for someone hotter."*
>
> *"I will never get over the pain I am in now."*
>
> *"I will never be happy."*

"*Nothing ever works out for me.*"

"*This is all my fault.*"

And so forth.

With the spread of how far our thoughts run at the occurrence of the triggering event, we can then challenge these thoughts and habits.

2. Challenging negative thoughts and habits

When an event like a break-up happens, it is normal to experience sadness, anger, and guilt. It is also praiseworthy to take responsibility for our role in the event, acknowledging our shortcomings and how they affect relationships.

However, we must subject these thoughts to scrutiny when we fall into repetitive and deteriorative patterns. This next step in CBT pokes holes at what we believe and why we believe it. The therapist may ask the heartbroken lover why they are convinced that the separation is their fault. Together, they journey into the patient's core beliefs about themselves and the world and how they shape automatic thoughts.

They consider that while we have some fault in the things happening around us, it takes two to tango. Is the patient so intent on blaming themselves while completely absolving the ex of their crimes? What is the evidence that the partner would have stayed if one did all that they thought they should have done? Is it reasonable to conclude broadly about their future based on one or a few events?

Asking these questions and examining the evidence presents the idea that perhaps our initial thinking is flawed, and we can now seek adjustments.

3. Replacing negative thoughts with positive ones

Reframing our thought process can be difficult, especially when dealing with deep-rooted beliefs that have developed over a long time. Yet it is not impossible.

When negative thoughts come under criticism and are found inaccurate, we must begin to replace them with positive ones. Replacement is not merely speaking positive and enthusiastic statements, nor does it entail ignoring the effects of a triggering situation.

On the contrary, it means that we open ourselves up to the awareness that mistakes do not make us bad people. We all have strengths and weaknesses- the latter does not diminish our self-worth but emphasizes our human nature.

At this point, we must not be unrealistic or merely peddle positivity and prosperity. Instead, we must tell ourselves what we know is within our grasp and is, therefore, valid.

For example, taking the thought, "I will never get over the pain I am in now," and instead saying, "I have no reason to be unhappy," diminishes the role of our feelings about the situation. Grief is part of healing and needs to be allowed. Instead, consider reframing the thought, "I know this hurts now, and that's okay. It is proof of the depth of my emotion. I know that I will heal over time, and I will allow it."

4. Implementing new habits

As we reframe negative and introduce positive thoughts, we empower ourselves to implement new habits. When we allow the realization that we are not a loser for breaking up with someone, we then encourage productive habits- getting out of bed and changing out of the sweatpants and sweatshirts, going back to the things we enjoyed doing when we were in the relationship like our hobbies, going outside, etc.

As we shift our thoughts, we can change how we feel and are more confident in ourselves and our choices. Interestingly, as we adjust our habits, we reinforce the new thoughts, boosting our mood.

Similarly, new habits that differ from our previous predispositions create an enormous sense of achievement and control. Imagine zip-lining across the XLine Dubai Marina a few ways down the road when you can hardly picture yourself on the rooftop of a ten-floor building today.

Remember that forming new thought patterns and habits takes time, so implementation should focus more on the progress and allow the time it would take.

Setting Goals

Life is interesting in that the entire human race experiences the same motions. We feel love and grief, courage and fear, motivation and despair. At the same time, every experience is as different as the next. Two people may sit next to each other at a party and talk to the same people but have entirely different experiences. Siblings in the same house, under the same parents for years, could tell varying stories about their shared lives.

For this reason, setting personal goals is crucial for a successful CBT program. Even if we both desired to be less anxious at work, the manifestation would vary.

In this next section, we will consider how you view various aspects of your life now, the issues causing you unrest, and the changes you want to make.

First, think about why you picked up this book. What were you looking for? What pushed you to go looking? How long have you had these concerns? How frequent are they?

Put down your thoughts in the space below.

_____

_____

_____

_____

_____

_____

_____

_____

The S in SWOT Analysis

We tend to focus on our weaknesses, especially when we are struggling. Yet we also have strengths, and these keep us grounded and carry us through difficulties. Our strengths are a powerful source of motivation, and being mindful of them can help to balance our inner being.

Think about your strengths. What are you good at? What comes naturally to you? What do the people in your life (your family, friends, colleagues, etc) appreciate about you?

Note them down below. Make the list as extensive as possible. If you'd like, ask someone that knows you well and cares about you to share what they see as your strong qualities.

_____

_____

_____

_____

_____

_____

_____

_____

The Facets of Your Life

Every human being has numerous matters in mind at any given moment. A random woman in traffic will probably think about her kids, whether her husband took his lunch to work, the colleagues she shares a cubicle with, that angry manager awaiting her report, the school PTA fundraising, etc.

Each of these facets contributes to our mental and physical wellbeing, and we shall look at them in turn as you review how your life is going.

1. Education and career/ business

Work provides a sense of meaning and achievement. When we are unhappy with our careers, we are likely to suffer a measure of dissatisfaction. Likewise, our work may suffer when we are in distress. Disorders like anxiety and depression cause concentration difficulties and fatigue and may limit productivity and efficiency.

How is your work going? Are you happy with what you do daily? Do you find meaning in what you do? Do you enjoy the dynamics with your colleagues? Are you able to handle the workload? Can you balance work and other responsibilities?

Consider too, how your mental health is affecting your work. Do you struggle to concentrate on your tasks or procrastinate? Do you avoid situations that may put you on the spot, like making presentations or speaking at meetings? As you note the observations in the space below, consider any other aspects affecting your professional life.

2. Financial health

Financial instability is a significant source of stress. Research indicates that during the COVID pandemic, the mental health of the unemployed and those in financial crises was worse than the general population (Fancourt et al., 2021). These studies also found that even before the pandemic, these groups still suffered accelerated stress, anxiety, and depression compared to the general population (Arends, 2015).

How is your money situation? Are you comfortable in your role as a provider, either for yourself or your family? Are you frustrated whenever the bills are due? Are you able to put away savings and make investments? Is your mental health affecting your motivation to be productive and earn a living?

Put down your thoughts below.

_____

_____

_____

_____

_____

_____

_____

_____

3. Relationships

We are social creatures that thrive in relationships and community. Our relationships with our parents, children, partners, and friends influence our satisfaction and dissatisfaction. For example, it is pretty telling that many therapy patients often have underlying issues from their childhood impacting their present problems and reactions.

a. Family

Think about your relationship with your family and the different roles you play. You may simultaneously be a parent, child, sibling, or spouse. How do you feel about the people in your life? What is going well with each of these relationships?

Are there stressors or conflicts? Is anyone going through something that is affecting the whole family?

Is your mental health affecting your capacity to play your roles? For example, as a parent, you are your children's provider and nurturer. Are you able to perform your duties healthily? Similarly, how does your family affect your mental health and well-being? Do you enjoy spending time with your family members? Are you able to spend time alone?

Share your thoughts below.

_____

_____

_____

_____

_____

_____

_____

b. Friends

Now, think about the friends you have and the role you play as a friend. Do you have and prefer many friends or a handful? Are you able to confide in people that you trust about various matters? Do you get to spend adequate time with your friends and do what you'd like? Are there strained friendships that may be causing unrest? Are the things you are mentally dealing with affecting your comradeships and vice versa?

Note your observations below.

_____

_____

_____

_____

_____

_____

_____

_____

_____

_____

c. The community

Finally, think about your role in the community. Do you feel a sense of belonging within your community? Do you share the general concerns and efforts to improve the community? Do you play any active roles, say, coaching a local team or joining the local watch? Do you enjoy the interactions you have with the people around you? Do you have and enjoy your privacy?

List your observations below.

_____
_____
_____
_____
_____
_____
_____
_____
_____

4. Physical health

Our body is the vessel carrying the mind- therefore, its health influences internal well-being.

a. General health

Are you concerned about your physical well-being? Do you manage any chronic issues like diabetes? How well do you know your body?

_____

_____

_____

_____

_____

_____

_____

_____

b. Exercise and physical activity

Do you undertake regular physical activities like walking, climbing stairs rather than taking the elevator, etc? Do you have a workout routine? Are you comfortable with your body? Do you enjoy any activities that feel more effortless, e.g., swimming or dancing?

_____

_____

c. Rest and sleep

Do you get enough sleep daily? Are you sleeping too little or too much? Do you have a regular sleeping pattern? Are you experiencing any challenges sleeping? Do you feel well-rested when you wake up? Do things like noisy cars, neighbors, pets, or kids affect your sleep?

Do you get other forms of rest? Can you relax after work, on weekends, or with friends and family?

5. Hobbies / personal development

Extra-curricular activities like hobbies tap into our creative and artistic sides.

Do you enjoy your hobbies? Do you get to do these fun activities as often as you'd like? Can you do them on bleak days, or is it hard to get the motivation? Do you work on projects like learning an instrument or language by self-motivation or nudging from others?

6. Values

Our values are what guide our beliefs and actions. They create in us a sense of purpose and influence our decisions.

What qualities motivate you? What ideals matter to you, e.g., family relationships, loyalty, respect, etc.?

What principles do you extend to others, and what do you expect of them? Does your mental health affect how you view what is important to you?

What are your Goals?

At this point, we can now define your specific goals.

Review all that you have noted above. Some thoughts may have been positive: Your good relationships and what is going well, great co-workers, etc. Think about how these made you feel: Grateful? Joyful? Supported? Loved?

Some observations may have been on the other end of the spectrum: Financial instability, physical health concerns, etc.

Consider how these made you feel too: Sad? Overwhelmed? Anxious?

Highlight the significant elements of each section. What would you like to be different by the end of this workbook? Think about how you want to feel and activities that you would like to get on.

While on this activity, focus on your goals, not what *you think you should achieve* or what you think someone else wants. They ought to be valuable to you to be meaningful. No particular number of goals is mandatory, but they should be manageable.

You can make them broad statements that we will dig into in later sections.

_____

_____

_____

_____

Dialogue Box:

SMART Goals

Remember that goals are more meaningful when they are SMART:

a. **Specific**- try to answer the questions, 'who, what, when, where, and why' to make the objective as straightforward as possible. For example, 'spend more time with my wife and kids' could become, 'Dedicate Friday evenings for movie night or game night with my wife and kids.'

b. **Measurable**- try to answer the questions, 'How much?' or 'How many?' For example, 'get enough sleep' could become 'get 7-8 hours of sleep every night.'

c. **Achievable**- set goals that are within reach. While challenging milestones can be a valuable source of motivation, too difficult tasks may be frustrating and demoralizing. Consider building on the goals instead, making each successive milestone more challenging than the last.

d. **Realistic-** be as practical as possible and consider the variables affecting execution. Spending three hours at the gym may be a tall order with a full-time job. Half an hour of intensive exercise would be more practical with this schedule.

e. **Time-bound-** specify a timeline for the milestones. Deadlines help keep you in check and provide a basis for evaluation of progress.

As we dig into CBT techniques for various disorders, we will refine the goals listed above, making it as SMART as possible.

Practicing CBT on Your Own

Not everyone goes the therapy way. You may have flipped open this workbook intending to go on a solo journey to wellness. While therapy is effective and recommended, particularly in cases of extreme distress, self-practice can still be adequate and sometimes more impactful.

Not everyone is comfortable opening up about their innermost thoughts and beliefs and they may have trouble sharing with their therapist. Moreover, the cost of therapy may be unaffordable vis-a-vis self-work and tools like this workbook.

So, how do you make the most of CBT when practicing independently?

1. Learn mindfulness

Tools like breathing exercises and meditation help to center the mind and take stock of the present and recurring thoughts. Mindfulness encourages observing thoughts and feelings without the judgment or criticism that would typically prompt further unhelpful spirals. It also helps to keep the attention on the present rather than dwelling on the past or worrying about the future.

As we become more mindful, we can nurture self-compassion and self-acceptance, which are crucial for our mental and emotional well-being. As we develop awareness of our thoughts and emotions, we become more aware of the feelings of others, helping us to be more compassionate towards them as well.

2. Develop self-compassion

Either as a result of our upbringing or socialization, we tend to be so hard on ourselves when in distress and for our shortcomings. We call ourselves names and hold ourselves to an impossible standard, chastising our actions and declaring multiple *'if only's.'*

Yet it is easier to work from the point of self-compassion. It is easier to set out knowing that we are deeply flawed like the next guy, which is not catastrophic. It is freeing to realize how flawed we are because we can work on ourselves with authenticity.

We must be compassionate when picking apart our unhelpful patterns and even more so when putting ourselves together anew. We may have the strongest intentions to change but only sometimes succeed: Only self-compassion can walk us through this block and allow us to change continuously, even if not immediately.

3. **Be aware of your limitations**

   Self-compassion helps us to accept our limitations. But we must be aware of these limitations to know how far we can stretch. This awareness is vital because it points us to the problematic areas of work and focuses on how to address them. We can set realistic goals and effective coping strategies and identify appropriate problem-solving tools. Moreover, we avoid the pitfalls of exaggerated expectations and resulting frustration and demotivation.

4. **Find support**

   Even without a therapist, support is essential when undergoing a CBT exercise. The therapy reveals much about yourself, which can be difficult to bear alone. Moreover, a support system keeps you in check and prevents you from relegating the work to the back burner or forgetting about it.

   Be careful when seeking support and establish places where you feel safe and heard without unhelpful criticism. Friends and family are always an immediate and robust pillar of love, compassion, and encouragement. Alternatively, find online communities with people who share your journey and help keep you on track.

5. **Make self-care a priority**

   Self-care is critical to the success of CBT. Make activities like exercise, healthy eating, adequate sleep, and rest fundamental components of your daily routine. Proper self-care helps to manage the problems associated with mental health symptoms, reduce stress, and promote improved well-being. Additionally, self-care allows one to practice CBT tools like relaxation techniques, communication, and problem-solving. As we improve with continued self-care, we become more resilient and capable of handling these same challenges and our emotions in the future.

Self-care need not be expensive or over the top. Simple habits like walking or establishing a balcony garden are a butterfly effect for much greater reward.

In this chapter, we examined where to begin a CBT program. We reviewed the facets of your life that impacted your mental health and drew a list of goals. In the next chapter, we shall look at the distortions driving negative thoughts and lay the foundation for the helpful tools we can employ for a more positive life.

Common Cognitive Distortions

Knowing yourself is the beginning of all wisdom.

- Aristotle (n.d.)

In the previous chapter, we considered the different facets of daily life that influence our mood and behavior. We observed the good bits to be grateful for and the not-so-great elements that need work. We then discussed how to use these observations to set the goals you would like to achieve by the end of this workbook.

This chapter will sharpen our awareness of self and others to catch negative thoughts that brew mood and behavior shifts. We will then discuss the common cognitive distortions that spur these thoughts.

By the end of this chapter, it will be easier to see negative thoughts as they arrive and understand the malformed internal setup that may automatically cultivate these thoughts. The new awareness will then allow the next level of change, which involves rationally questioning these thoughts for positive reframing.

So, how do we identify a negative thinker, especially when we are the culprit?

The Signs and Symptoms of Negative Thinking

Have you talked with a friend or relative about any random topic, their personal life, the weather, COVID, and the recession, and found yourself quietly thinking, 'Wow, this person is quite negative'? They constantly find and lead with a negative thing or conclusion to every subject, even if they are not necessarily rude or sarcastic.

We all have moments of anxiety, sadness, and despair, which can become detrimental when unchecked and unbalanced. Moreover, even with the most positive predispositions, we can become infected by the next person's negative energy. This exposure to unpleasant vibes may diminish our quality of life, limiting our capacity to face each day with zeal.

Awareness means we can identify negative sentiments as soon as they come up within ourselves and others, so we can arrest how we react to them.

What are some of the signs of a negative thinker?

1. They are chronic worriers

Negative thinkers cannot help but worry. It is difficult for them to fathom things going well. Instead, they constantly wonder, 'What if I lose my job?' 'What if I never get better?' 'What if I fail again?' 'What if the economy crashes?'

The constant worry keeps them in a loop of distressing emotions like frustration, fear, helplessness, and defeat, affecting their daily life and overall well-being.

While we are all prone to worry, especially during difficult periods, the negative person takes it up several notches. For them, a good day or positive outlook is almost as rare as a blue moon.

Do you know a chronic worrier, say at home or work, in your immediate environment?

What are some of the things they constantly worry out loud about?

_____

_____

_____

_____

_____

_____

_____

2. They are pessimists

The negative thinker sees the glass as half-empty or even fully empty. Their jobs will be under appraisal, and they say, 'I just know I'll get a negative review.'

The sky will get cloudy while on a picnic, and they muse, 'It will probably rain and ruin our day.'

They will get a bad break and say, 'Getting out of this is impossible.'

It is challenging for such a person to see the possibility of a good outcome. Even when the odds are favorable, they still find ways to see and lean toward the worst possible scenarios.

3. They are over-complainers

People with a gloomy outlook on life complain about everything. They complain that it is too hot in the summer, too wet in the rainy season, and too cold in the winter. They find fault in eating out and ordering in. They are displeased when something is too expensive and when it is too cheap.

Negative thinkers blame everyone for their troubles and conclude everything is against them. The universe must especially hate them on the days that cars slosh puddle water all over their work clothes at 9 am!

Detrimentally, they may fail to account for other factors that determine progress, like hard work and the influence of coincidences.

4. They do not / cannot limit their exposure to bad news

If you want to hear bad news, turn on the television. Calamities are always going on in one part of the world or another. Wars, drought, famine, school shootings- the list is endless.

A negative person can't help but soak all these in like a sponge. Yet research indicates that constant exposure to negative information impacts our mental health. In a study on two undergraduate student groups, both experienced heightened state anxiety and total mood disturbance (TMD) and lowered positive affect after exposure to a random 15-minute newscast. This effect reversed in one group when the respondents were taken through relaxation exercises after the newscast but remained the same in the latter group (Szabo & Hopkinson, 2007).

Psychologists suggest that continuous intake of violent media accelerates the symptoms of anxiety, depression, and stress. Anxiety, fear, or sadness may silently make you more attuned to negative information, further strengthening the destructive loop.

Have you been exposed to constant disturbing news on the TV or social media lately? Did they dampen your spirits or make you more worried than usual? Were you more stressed after watching the news than you were before?

Think about it for a few minutes and note what you felt, thought, or did after this exposure. If you are unsure about previous experiences, be more observant of your automatic reactions for the next few days or weeks and note them below.

_____

_____

_____

_____

_____

_____

_____

_____

5. They are defensive and closed off

A negative thinker is likely to think poorly of any interaction. They may assume they will be put on the spot and embarrassed, have nothing valuable to say, are not interesting enough, etc.

As a result, they may avoid engagements that especially nudge them to speak out. They may sit at the back of meetings and keep silent, even if they have impactful opinions. When provoked, they may become defensive and even more closed off. Ironically, they may then use the next person's reaction to their behavior (say displeasure, anger, dismissiveness, etc.) to reinforce why they should remain closed off in the future.

6. They are easily offended

Negative people easily misconstrue innocent remarks as offensive or rude. They tend to be brittle and see the worst possible thing you could have meant by any statement.

For example, Clark and Lois are in a group of friends, and Lois talks incessantly. Clark asks Lois to pipe down. Lois immediately goes glum, thinking,

> *"I must be embarrassing myself."*
>
> *"He must hate me now for being so chatty."*
>
> *"I should never speak at parties."*

In actuality, Clark may have meant that she allows the rest of the party to get a word in, not that her speaking is a problem.

7. The future does not excite them

The uncertainty about the future unsettles the negative thinker. They are more likely to ruminate on how wrong things could go than the chances of a positive outcome. They may think about the coming days with anxiety or dread, almost convinced they will fail the test even though they studied, getting back into the dating pool will be too difficult, and they cannot meet someone new. They may believe they cannot find better work than their current awful job and leaving will be useless.

Sadly, such thoughts take away the novelty of life. They prevent us from truly appreciating the high and low tides and the gifts each season presents. They block our mind from the possibility that while uncertainty can be scary, it just as equally holds the probability for great tidings.

8. They stay within their comfort zone

Part of the motions a negative thinker grapples with include resistance to change and challenges. They are perhaps afraid of failure, of getting embarrassed in the quest for growth, or of the required exertion. Perhaps they believe that they do not deserve a higher place in life. They may struggle to conceptualize the benefits of leaping into higher growth levels.

As a result, they prefer to keep the boat as steady as possible, avoiding the situations that would rock the vessel. They do not jump into the waves below for fear of drowning. They do not build oars to paddle to unexplored islands for fear of dangerous creatures and men. They do not jump onto larger ships for fear of putting one leg out of the boat and risking overturning.

However, while the comfort zone is, as the name suggests, comfortable, remaining there effectively keeps us from growing into stronger, healthier beings. We will not know if we can stay afloat, learn to swim, or ride the wave if we never jump into the water. We risk not finding sustenance if we never reach out to new land. We miss greater stability if we never dare to climb aboard bigger vessels.

Are there any areas in your life that would represent growth but which you feel resistant about? Perhaps the thought of venturing out makes you nervous. Perhaps your confidence wavers at the idea of change. A voice may argue for staying in the same state, even though growth has apparent benefits.

Share your thoughts below:

_____

_____

_____

_____

_____

_____

_____

_____

_____

_____

9. They are underachievers

You must leave your comfort zone to discover the depth of your potential. Negative thinkers resist challenges, withdrawing from things that would accelerate their thoughts and feelings of fear, inadequacy, and self-doubt.

It seems reasonable to avoid situations that cause such distress. However, the sacrifice to 'feel safe' is immobility- without motion, there can be no achievement. Ironically, negative thinkers may feel left behind by their peers even though they cannot bring themselves to push beyond the safety net.

10. They are 'but' speakers

Negative thinkers cannot help including the word 'but' in their statements. Of course, it is natural to find fault with things and to acknowledge that imperfections exist. Yet the Negatron will almost go out of their way to find blemishes even where the good qualities are in plenty. Moreover, they fixate on these imperfections and may disregard the good traits in a situation or person, carrying a somewhat blurred perception.

For example, Edith visits Larry's house for the first time and says, "This house is nice, but I bet the ones on the upper floors are better."

Mitchell buys a new car, and his colleague remarks, "This would have been so much more amazing in a different color."

11. They are energy-suckers

You cannot give what you do not have. People with a dull outlook have difficulty harnessing positive energy and sharing it. Instead, their off-putting vibes may seep into the people around them, snuffing out the light.

My friend got married a few years ago. When planning the wedding, she mentioned a friend she'd wanted to have as a bridesmaid but changed her mind. My friend said, "I just couldn't have a conversation with her without feeling drained afterward! Something always was going on with her that demanded attention- some drama she got herself into, fights with her baby-daddy, issues at work. Without realizing it, I became irritable and snapped at my fiancé and sisters several times. It was exhausting. I couldn't have that energy around my wedding."

12. They often see the dark clouds in your sunny sky

Perhaps quite annoyingly, negative thinkers often rain on your parade. They almost cannot receive exciting news without putting a damper on things. You may say to such a person that you're moving to Italy, and their first response is how dirty the cities are and how hard it is to get a job. You may say that you're going back to school for your Master's degree, and they remark on how expensive such a venture is. You may want to get a cat, and they remind you that the creatures are believed to be involved in witchcraft. It is not enough for them to wish you well- they must add words of caution or *warning*.

Negative persons may come off as intentionally unkind or mean. In truth, however, they may not even be aware that they are being negative. They may lack the power to turn it off where they are aware, not knowing where the button or the controls are.

This is because we are all susceptible to cognitive distortions that adversely impact our reactions to people and situations.

Common Cognitive Distortions

My student Katrina and I had tea a week after the class test. Unlike her usual cheery self, she had been more sullen in the days after getting their tests back. She was distracted and did not participate in the class discussions.

Over tea and scones, I led her into the conversation about her results, how she felt, and what she thought. She said, "I feel like a failure. I should have studied more. Maybe I would have done better if I hadn't gone to the movies that weekend."

I pointed out that she had, in fact, performed exceptionally and had the third-highest score on a test that was quite challenging. At this, she added, "But I was not the best in the class. And I did poorer than in previous tests. I suck. Maybe I won't pass the compulsory exam and get my certificate."

It occurred to me that perhaps Katrina was operating from a few cognitive distortions that caused her to belittle her exemplary performance. In truth, she was one of the most focused students, and I did not doubt that she would do well. She had evidence of all the tests she had done so far and her performance, yet this one event caused her to feel inadequate.

After her let-out, I dug into my hypothesis, beginning with an elaboration of cognitive distortions. These errors prompt irrational assumptions and a distorted view of the world. They often catalyze a pessimistic worldview, causing negative thoughts and emotions. Left unchecked, they can have detrimental effects like low self-esteem, accelerated anxiety, and depression.

I then explained that these cognitive errors are not a rare occurrence. Many of us unknowingly gravitate towards one or more of these fallacies owing to our past negative experiences, inaccurate beliefs, and malformed thought patterns.

Moreover, they are not indicators that anything is wrong with us. On the contrary, they manifest what we know and have always known and, therefore, can be reshaped as we increase awareness.

We then went through the distortions below, picking out those resonating most with her.

1. Always being right

This distortion creates the idea that we must always be right and that being wrong is unacceptable. The cognitive error may cause us to believe that being right is more significant than what others feel, admitting when we've made mistakes or fairness.

Subsequently, the effects of this distortion include inflated ego, dysfunctional relationships, and challenges with accountability and, therefore, growth.

2. Blaming

Taking responsibility for faults can be a hurdle. Similarly, a person with this cognitive error tends to assign responsibility to others whenever things do not go their way. Otherwise, they blame others for making them feel or act a particular way.

Consider a lover that blames their partner for every problem. They may likely think:

> "If my partner spent more time with me, I wouldn't have to fight to get attention."

> "If my partner understood me, I wouldn't cheat on them."

Blaming is dangerous because it blinds us to our faults and contributions to situations that may sever relationships. It also leaves our stability at the mercy of others, relying on them to be happy and thriving. No one is responsible for our actions or feelings but ourselves.

3. Catastrophizing / magnifying or minimizing

Catastrophizing is where one tends to inflate the chance of an adverse occurrence while underestimating their capacity to handle it. They magnify the possible negative consequences, often assuming the worst-case scenario in situations that are not as catastrophic as imagined.

For example, believing you will lose your job because you made a mistake.

On the other hand, minimizing involves diminishing positive qualities such as a healthy personal trait or an academic achievement.

Both catastrophizing and minimizing may lead to low confidence, the fear of failure, and feelings of anxiety and dread.

4. Control fallacies

Control fallacies embody the belief that all events happening to a person are either a result of external forces or entirely because of their actions. It takes the 'one or the other' stance and ignores the reality that a collection of variables can trigger circumstances.

Floki is one of the main characters in the History Channel drama TV series Vikings and makes for an interesting assessment of the control fallacy (Tyler, 2022). He is devoted to the Norse gods like Odin and Thor and lives his whole life aiming to please them. While the rest of the Northmen are similarly devout to their religion, Floki takes the absolute stance that everything happening to them must be the will and the fault of the gods to bless or punish them.

He also believes that his shortcomings are enough to inflict the wrath of the gods upon the entire earldom of Kattegat and blames himself when they are unsuccessful in their raids. Similarly, he blames the dead Christian Priest Athelstan (*who lived among them for years as a friend and advisor to their King, Ragnar. Floki himself murders Athelstan as a sacrifice to the gods and to purify the people from religious pluralism*) when the Vikings fail to conquer Paris and instead suffer their most tremendous loss yet.

While belief is undoubtedly powerful, Floki fails to consider the variables determining the victor in any war, such as weaponry, armor, and battle strategies.

5. Emotional reasoning

Emotional reasoning is the belief that if we feel a particular way, then it must be true. We are told to follow our heart and trust its leading. Yet the heart's motions can be misplaced due to our cognitive errors.

If Leslie feels unattractive, she may think that she is, even if the mirror says otherwise.

Derek may feel like a loser because things didn't work out as he hoped and label himself a loser, even if this is just one setback.

While it can be challenging to look past how we feel, emotional reasoning is irrational and unstable because it leaves us subject to the motions of our feelings which rise and fall like ocean tides. On the days Leslie feels radiant and attractive, she thinks she is. Yet she is the same face and the same body in each situation.

6. Filtering

Filtering is a distortion where a person focuses on some aspects of a situation while ignoring others. In this case, they tend to focus on the negative elements of a situation or their life and ignore the positive qualities.

Filtering can be detrimental because it makes it difficult to see the bright side of things even when good things surround us.

For example, a bad breakup or separation from a lover is undoubtedly painful and takes a while to heal. However, a person with this type of distortion is likely to obsess over this event even if they have the company of good friends and family and a great job. They are likely to dwell on the qualities about them that led to the separation and ignore the qualities that make them lovable to other people and appreciated at work.

7. Overgeneralization

Overgeneralization takes a single negative occurrence and uses it as proof for a broad conclusion.

For example, failing one test and concluding that you must be a failure in the subject, or meeting one unpleasant company rep and assuming that the whole organization has unpleasant staff.

Overgeneralization is damaging because it often leads to despair and low self-esteem.

8. Global labeling

Global labeling is an extreme form of generalization that involves drawing a global negative conclusion from a single event.

For instance, failing one job interview and concluding that you are unemployable, or having a deficiency in one aspect and figuring that you are a total failure in everything.

Global labeling can cause immense self-doubt, low self-esteem, and depression. Yet it is false because no one is defined by one event and lacks weaknesses or shortcomings. Instead, we are all a sum of every event happening to us and because of us. Some events bring out our highest selves, while others point to areas of improvement.

9. Heaven's reward fallacy

Heaven's reward fallacy is the expectation that any act of self-denial or sacrifice deserves a reward. This way, we expect a reward for our good deeds and may suffer bitterness when there is none.

However, the idea of a reward for good deeds is erroneous because it does not tally with reality. In reality, self-sacrifice may yield zero rewards. Bad things may happen to good people. Good things may happen to bad people. The sun shines, and the rain pours on the just and the unjust (*Matthew 5:45*, n.d.)

10. Jumping to conclusions

An individual with a propensity to jump to conclusions often makes judgments without gathering all the evidence. They are likely to make hasty assumptions without collecting all the data that would allow them to make an informed decision.

For example, Myra encounters a stern manager at the Monday morning meeting who criticizes her performance and concludes that the manager must not like her.

In this case, there is no actual evidence, except that the manager poked at her work, which ideally is his job.

Jumping to conclusions can lead to hurried and erroneous choices that may damage your social and professional life.

11. Mind-reading

Much like jumping to conclusions, mind-reading assumes we know what someone must be thinking, feeling, or intending without actual facts. Mind reading tends to occur when feelings of insecurity, inadequacy, or anxiety arise.

For example, Lisa wakes up to find her boyfriend Ethan already out of bed without saying good morning like he usually does.

He hardly talks to her all day, and Lisa assumes he must be upset with her.

In this case, there could be tons of reasons why Ethan is uncharacteristic but which have nothing to do with Lisa. He could be upset about work or that his favorite basketball team lost.

Mind-reading can cause negative assumptions and communication challenges and harm relationships.

12. Personalization

Personalization is the irrational belief that my actions have an influence on events and other people and that I have an active role in the awful things happening around me, even when they have nothing to do with me.

This cognitive error makes one believe that they are responsible for other people's happiness or suffering. Personalization takes on a weight that accelerates anxiety and depression.

To illustrate, a mother blaming herself for her child's illness may think, "If I took better care of him, he wouldn't get sick'.

But this is a distorted thought process because kids are prone to illness occasionally, and a parent cannot monitor everything they do and every nook and cranny they fit into.

13. Polarized thinking

Polarized thinking is the all-or-nothing distortion that allows no room for convolution or variation. It takes the stance that life is all black or white and views people, circumstances, and events on this extreme measure.

Polarized thinking may prompt the assertion that one is either a total failure or total success, leaving no room for the idea that you may be naturally skilled in one thing and unskilled in another.

I remembered an old episode of Cartoon Network's, The Grim Adventures of Billy and Mandy, where a little demon poses the riddle to Mandy, "What is black and blue, and red all over?" (Dr. Pizzazz, 2021) The nuances in each situation we encounter, and the diversity and complexity of our being, make 'life' a valid answer to the riddle.

At the very least, life is numerous shades of gray, which ought to permit us to judge ourselves less rigidly and therefore undo unhelpful thoughts and emotions.

14. 'Shoulds'

The 'shoulds' cognitive distortion exhibits implicit or explicit rules we believe our behavior and others must adhere to to be acceptable or successful. It is a form of all-or-nothing distortion.

For example, making a mistake and thinking, ' I should have known better.' or 'I should have prepared better.

The strict sense of 'should' creates guilt when we break our rules and frustration or anger at others when they break them. It can prompt disappointment and resentment, yet life is anything but rigid, and the rules limit our willingness to bend and fold and therefore evolve.

ACTIVITY

Did you see one or more distortions that Katrina might embody? List them below with a short elaboration of why.

_____

_____

_____

_____

_____

_____

_____

_____

_____

ACTIVITY

Now that you understand the distortions that influence how we feel and act, take these next few moments to consider some of the irrational thoughts you have held in the past.

Go back to the distressing event you mapped out when working on the CBT diagram. Remember how you felt and what you did, and then review the random thoughts that prompted these reactions.

To recap, the CBT cycle loops thoughts, feelings, and behavior, as below:

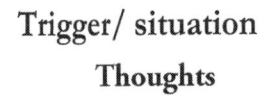

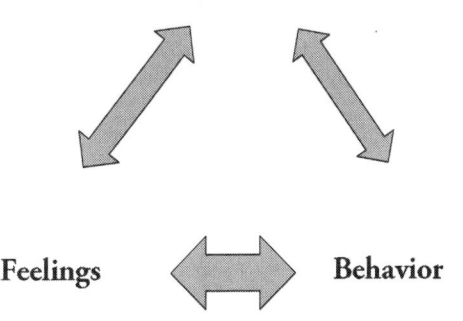

Trigger/ situation
Thoughts

Feelings ⟷ **Behavior**

Consider what you thought then, now reviewing the potential distortions that could have led to these thoughts.

Be as honest and exhaustive as possible, and write them down in the space below. Don't worry if you cannot immediately identify the distortions. We shall come back to the distortions severally over the workbook, and they will be more apparent by the end.

_____

_____

_____

_____

_____

_____

_____

_____

_____

In this chapter, we have covered the signs and symptoms of a negative thinker. We also uncovered the common cognitive distortions that may spur such unhelpful thought patterns. Cognitive distortions are normal, and we all suffer from our fair share depending on our environment and socialization. However, too many distortions lead to an imbalanced flow of negative thoughts, triggering stress and disorders like anxiety and depression.

In the following two chapters, we shall unpack anxiety and depression and the tools that can help manage their symptoms.

Understanding Anxiety and Depression

Nobody realizes that some people expend enormous energy merely to be normal.

- Albert Camus (n.d.)

Cognitive distortions develop from irrational assumptions and breed negative automatic thoughts. These distortions stem from our socialization, taking root in our beliefs about ourselves, others, and the world.

Cognitive distortions may have us apportioning ourselves all the blame in an unfortunate situation, even where we have little or no personal affiliation to the event. They may wear a polarized hat, taking life from an all-or-nothing perspective and drawing extreme conclusions.

The previous chapter explored the diverse forms that common cognitive distortions take. These irrational thoughts become apparent in how we behave. Negative thinkers exhibit chronic worry, struggle to break out of their comfort zone, are over-sensitive to criticism, and take on a pessimistic view.

This chapter looks at anxiety and depression, two disorders largely aggravated by the cycle of negative thoughts, emotions, and behavior. Anxiety and depression are common and potentially detrimental disorders, with the World Health Organization estimating that 300 million people suffer from depression worldwide (2023).

Anxiety comes in the shape of specific phobias, panic disorders, and social anxiety disorders, prompting avoidance behavior that may diminish our quality of life. Depression creates a clouded perception of self and may lower self-confidence, esteem, and willingness to participate in life and thrive.

As we get into it, let us join Megan, who recently took the two-hour bus to her parent's home.

Anxiety at Play

> Megan sits in the shuttle for the two-hour drive to her folks' place. She sits by the window as she always prefers, so she can crack it open and get some air without bothering the person next to her or behind her to do it. She has a book in her bag, and her phone and air pods are fully charged.
>
> The bus exits the terminal slowly, makes its way through traffic, and is soon out on the open highway. As soon as the city is behind them, the driver picks up speed but remains within the speed limit. Though he is at par with other vehicles on the road, the driver sticks to his lane and does not rush to overtake other vehicles or squeeze his way through tight spaces. He plays soft music and chats with the bus conductor, who leans against a railing.

Within a few minutes, Megan starts to feel the usual discomfort. Her armpits are suddenly moist as the sweat sticks to her shirt. Her heartbeat picks up, and she draws long breaths to steady her heart. Her hands are sweaty, and her stomach starts turning.

Her mind races as she thinks,

"Is this driver going too fast?"

"What if we lose control and plunge over a cliff or collide with another car?"

"Is this safety belt actually safe" (she surreptitiously tugs at it)

She looks around at the other passengers. Some are laughing as they chat with their friends. Many are on their phones. Some are asleep already. No one seems particularly concerned that the driver is driving recklessly.

Megan draws in another long breath and takes out her book. She tries to read for a while but keeps glancing outside every few minutes. She finally takes out her phone and plays music softly, then leans back on her seat and closes her eyes.

She contemplates how often this has happened every time she gets in a car, especially when traveling long distances. She wasn't always like this. As far back as she can remember, she enjoyed road trips. However, since she got into an accident three years ago, she has been unable to relax in a moving vehicle. Her car had collided with another, and there had been shattered glass and explosive sounds. She wasn't injured, but several passengers had bangs and bruises, and one had to spend a few days at the hospital.

Though she was not hurt, it was a frightening experience, and she often replays it in her head when she travels.

She also avoids taking cars whenever possible, choosing to walk where she can and even where it is more than a stretch. She stopped driving and has not renewed her driver's license since it expired more than a year ago.

As she settles into the long drive, she hopes she will drift off and wake up just as they pull into the station at her destination.

When we encounter a real or perceived threat, the body kicks into the protective stress response. We can all relate to the beads of sweat just before a big presentation, the accelerated heartbeat in an accident, and the shortness of breath in the struggle to regain breath control. All these symptoms are the result of the body preparing for fight or flight and are instinctive indicators that keep us alive. While these episodes can be frequent given the everyday life stressors, they tend to be manageable, and the system regains calm quickly.

However, a person with an anxiety disorder frequently experiences episodes of intense and persistent fear or worry that can last a few minutes. The feelings of panic are hard to control and often out of proportion to the actual danger. An attack can last longer than a few minutes triggering further anxiety.

Anxiety disorders come in numerous forms, depending on the sources and triggers. While they can be challenging, treatment, including medication and therapy tools like CBT, can help.

The Main Types of Anxiety

1. Specific phobia

Specific phobia manifests as a heavy, often irrational fear of a particular object or situation. Consider the people afraid of heights, mice, or even the dark. Specific phobias are not uncommon and are as numerous as they are diverse.

A few specific phobias include:

PHOBIA	MEANING
Arachnophobia	The fear of spiders and other spider-like creatures or arachnids
Acrophobia	The fear of heights
Aerophobia	The fear of flying
Claustrophobia	The fear of tight or enclosed spaces
Cynophobia	The fear of dogs

Hemophobia	The fear of blood
Mysophobia	The fear of germs
Ophidiophobia	The fear of snakes
Trypanophobia	The fear of injections or needles

Can you think of any specific phobias you might experience?

_____

_____

2. Generalized Anxiety Disorder (GAD)

Generalized Anxiety Disorder manifests as constant and excessive worry about a myriad of people or events. GAD stretches out to multiple areas over a continual length of time.

As such, a person with GAD may worry about their job today, their relationship tomorrow, and their family next week. When work is worry-free, they will worry about their upcoming doctor's appointment and what the President said at the last conference.

GAD thus becomes a prolonged apprehension that affects the quality of daily life and overall well-being. The symptoms of GAD include:

- Difficulty concentrating on tasks
- Restlessness and irritability
- Muscle tension
- Sleep challenges
- Constant fatigue

3. Social Anxiety Disorder

Social anxiety disorder is an immense fear of social situations. It differs from specific phobias in that while specific phobias are based on fear of the consequences resulting from the thing happening, social anxiety takes the form of guesses.

It is the fear that we might make a fool of ourselves or be humiliated that assumes what other people must be thinking. Louis might sit through a work party with these thoughts going through his head:

> *"Is my shirt bland?"*
>
> *"Am I interesting, or are they listening just to be polite?"*
>
> *"Was that joke tacky?"*
>
> *"Can they see the sweat blotches through the shirt?"*

This spiral of thoughts will likely make Louis self-conscious, restless, and unable to ease into the crowd and have a good time. He may even miss the party next time, preferring to spend Friday evening at home or with the crowd he is used to.

4. Panic disorder

A panic disorder is where one experiences abrupt and repeated episodes of intense fear. These attacks are commonly a few minutes long and can strike at any moment and place, like while taking a walk, driving, or at a restaurant.

The disorder is characterized by other physical symptoms such as dizziness, shortness of breath, heart palpitations, and abdominal distress.

While many people can and have experienced panic attacks, experiencing these attacks is not a pointer to struggling with the disorder itself. Conditions like post-traumatic stress and substance use disorder may trigger panic attacks yet do not qualify as a panic disorder. However, a panic disorder can occur alongside other mental health disorders and can sometimes be challenging to diagnose and treat.

A panic attack signals a mental sense of impending danger, even without indicators of an actual threat. This signal shifts the body into protective mode, activating the automatic, often unconscious responses that occur as symptoms of an attack.

The mind spirals into figuring out what is wrong, and if it cannot find the trigger in the immediate external environment, then turns inwards, assuming a medical emergency. One may think they are experiencing a heart attack or stroke, which unfortunately only worsens the experience.

The manifestation of a panic attack includes:

- Chills
- Profuse sweating
- Shortness of breath
- Dizziness, lightheadedness, or faintness
- Tense muscles, which can cause trembling or shaking
- The fear/ feeling of loss of control
- A sense of detachment from reality
- Abdominal distress
- Headache and chest pain
- Numbness or a tingling sensation
- Accelerated heart rate

A person battling a panic disorder will repeatedly experience these unexpected attacks, often feeling anxiety between episodes. They may cause the person to constantly worry about the next attack's occurrence, developing phobias about where the attacks have happened or may happen. As a result, they may start avoiding places and situations like going to the store, driving on certain roads, or where they fear immediate help would be unavailable.

Sometimes, avoiding the places and situations that trigger the panic attacks may evolve into another anxiety disorder called agoraphobia.

5. Agoraphobia

Agoraphobia develops out of the instinct to avoid the places where panic attacks are likely. As such, it manifests as a fear of public places, especially crowded areas where an attack would draw attention or where help would not be immediately available.

Persons with agoraphobia are likely to avoid places like restaurants, movie theaters, shopping malls, and public transport. The renowned poet, Emily Dickinson, is believed to have suffered immense agoraphobia as she lived out most of her life as a recluse in her second-floor bedroom of the family home. During that time, she wrote more than 1500 poems, many speculating on life, nature, and death (Mondragon, n.d.).

A Cognitive-Behavioral Perspective of Anxiety

The thoughts of an anxious mind take on frantic connotations, supplying all the perceived notes about the threat. As such, a person with intense claustrophobia may automatically think, 'This space is too small to hold enough air' or 'What if I start suffocating?'

An acrophobic may think, 'What if I fall from this distance?' 'How sure am I that I am safe and the floor will not cave in?'

The accompanying emotions are what we may identify with easier. During a panic attack, one may feel intense fear, especially when accompanied by the dread of mortality.

The anxious person is likely to develop avoidance habits to eliminate the anxiety. The reasoning is that if they avoid situations that are probable triggers, then the alarm will not go off in the first place. Louis may avoid parties or social gatherings, attempting to keep the social anxiety at bay. An agoraphobic may avoid leaving the house for days or weeks.

As Megan rode that two-hour bus home, her thoughts and emotions probably looked something like this:

**Trigger/ situation:
Taking a bus ride**

Thoughts:

**What if we crash into another car?
Is this driver going too fast?**

Feelings:

Intense fear, dread.

Behavior:

Distracted
Unable to focus on a book
or relax into the music
Checking other passengers
and the safety belt

While it sounds good on paper to avoid the places and things that make you anxious, life becomes imbalanced if the behavior threatens your health or sustainability. If we avoid social situations, we deny ourselves the room to interact with others and build relationships. We miss the joys of surrounding ourselves with loved ones and coming up for air. If we evade crowded places, we deny ourselves simple pleasures like sitting in a theater for a movie or eating out and being part of an alive world.

Sometimes the overwhelming fear and dread can interfere with crucial parts of our livelihood. Anxiety disrupts focus and may diminish work productivity when chronic and unmanaged. Prolonged anxiety increases stress because the body is constantly in the fight-or-flight state. Stress accompanied by insufficient rest and resulting fatigue may then interfere with your physical health causing long-term problems like high blood pressure.

CBT tools introduce adjustments into the thought-emotion-behavior loop aiming to change the reaction to a trigger. The techniques work to alter automatic, fear-based thoughts and protective, avoidant behavior. Further, they help us accept that some variables are beyond our control but that we can control how we react to them and take charge of the elements within our grasp.

Suppose Megan was able to think, "I know that accidents are a scary thing, and there is no guarantee that I will arrive at my destination safely each time. However, I can also see that the driver is within the speed limit, not swerving dangerously or engaging in reckless behavior. I can trust that he is doing his best to get me home safely."

This thought may not wholly take away the anxiety, but it introduces the idea that while she cannot control what happens on the road, she can trust the person at the wheel, given the evidence he has presented. With this knowledge, she may lower the feelings of fear and dread allowing her to ease into an activity like reading or engaging her neighbor.

Perhaps her internal process may become something like this:

**Trigger/ situation:
Taking a bus ride**

Thoughts:

"I cannot control whether we get to our destination safely. However, I can trust that the driver is driving reasonably and will do his best to get me home."

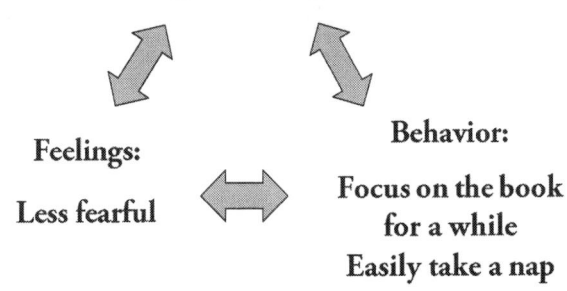

Feelings:

Less fearful

Behavior:

Focus on the book for a while
Easily take a nap

As she allows more thoughts like these and exposes herself back to the road slowly, she may be able to work through the anxiety built up after her harrowing experience and even gather the confidence to get back on the wheel.

ACTIVITY

Anxiety Triggers

What are some of the things that make you anxious? Perhaps it is standing in front of a crowd. Maybe getting stuck in the elevator sends your heart racing. Perhaps the sight of a lizard sends you up on the couch.

Think about the small and big things that trigger your anxiety. If you need help remembering, consider the signs of anxiety. Think back to moments that accelerate your heartbeat, cause muscle tension, lightheadedness, or any of the numerous symptoms.

Note these triggers below.

_____

_____

_____

_____

_____

_____

_____

_____

Understanding Depression

Depression is often described as a heavy cloud pressing upon the body, sapping the energy and sometimes the will to live. In season 2 of the American adult animated coming-of-age sitcom Big Mouth (2017), 13-year-old Jessi Glaser has been going through mental and emotional distress following the falling apart of her parents' marriage. She acts out by shoplifting, running away from home, doing drugs, and getting into an on-and-off casual relationship with her schoolmate. She is not as chatty as she was with her classmates before and does not participate in her usual school activities.

The show 'Big Mouth' addresses diverse issues in mental health, puberty, and sexuality. It uses creatures to depict shame (Lionel the Shame Wizard), anxiety (Tito the Anxiety Mosquito), ambition (gremlins), hormones (hormone monsters), and plenty more. In the season 2 finale, Jessi meets Depression Kitty, who takes control because Jessi (and her hormone monster) have been making things worse, trying to feel better.

Jessi agrees to go with Depression Kitty as she admits, "I am so tired of fighting and feeling bad." As they walk into the Depression Ward, Kitty asks, "Jessi, have you ever laid on your side facing away from the television listening to a Friends marathon? It's raining outside, and you're wearing double socks" (Salazar, 2018)

Depression is a mood disorder manifesting as continual sadness and a lack of interest in previously enjoyed activities. Jessi lays there with Depression Kitty for a while, away from everyone and with the heavy, furry cat pressing down upon her so she can hardly move. It takes hearing her friends look for her to wake up and want to fight her way out of the depression ward, and she eventually agrees to go for therapy.

Depression can start quietly and almost unnoticed and can be severely detrimental as isolation and despair deepen. Fortunately, treatment and therapeutic tools like CBT can help manage the various types of depression.

The Types of Depression

1. Major Depression

Major depression, or clinical depression, is the most common form of depression and affects a person's capacity to carry out their day-to-day activities. Like other mood disorders, it influences how a person thinks, feels, and acts.

When people struggle with clinical depression, they may likely lose their zeal for life. They experience prolonged sadness and lose interest in what they previously enjoyed. A delightful walk in the late afternoon sun becomes a reluctance to leave the house. Hobbies slip to the shelf and gather dust.

Other symptoms of major depression include:

- Disrupted sleep patterns
- Changes in appetite
- Energy loss
- Challenges concentrating on a task
- Strong feelings of guilt and worthlessness

The thoughts and emotions that spiral within are sometimes overwhelming to manage, and the mental agony accelerates the thoughts of death or suicide.

Clinical depression has varied causes and risk factors, making it sometimes difficult to diagnose. These factors include changes in one's brain chemistry, environment, genetic elements, and stressful situations. However, while stressful situations can trigger the disorder, not everyone that goes through a difficult situation and is affected by it will necessarily develop major depression. Moreover, the condition's symptoms will differ in every patient depending on its manifestation.

2. Persistent Depressive Disorder (PDD)

As the name suggests, persistent depressive disorder (dysthymia) is a prolonged form of depression. Clinical depression occurs in shorter periods- a patient may experience high and low periods, even without treatment.

However, PDD is more chronic and lasts up to two years, with a person experiencing depressive motions for most of that time. It is a low-grade condition that may manifest more mildly than major depression and with fewer symptoms.

The possible symptoms of PDD include:

- Low interest in activities
- Fatigue
- Concentration challenges
- Feelings of despair
- Low self-esteem

Even though PDD will be diagnosed with fewer symptoms compared to major depression, the former is still detrimental to overall well-being and affects the capacity to undertake daily activities.

Like major depression, the risk elements for PDD include biological, genetic, and environmental factors. Moreover, people more prone to depression are at a higher risk of PPD than those who are not.

3. Postpartum depression (PPD)

Postpartum depression is a problematic condition that may affect women after childbirth. It gives rise to intense feelings of anxiety, tiredness, and sadness. Other physical symptoms of PPD include muscle tension and headaches.

PPD can last for weeks or months and can be consequential to the woman's ability to care for herself and her child.

The potential causes of PPD are a combination of the physical and hormonal changes that occur during and after pregnancy.

Hormones like estrogen, progesterone, and cortisol drop significantly after childbirth, causing an immediate emotional shift. Additional triggers for the disorder include erratic sleep patterns, lifestyle changes, and isolation, which come with caring for a newborn.

4. Premenstrual dysphoric disorder (PMDD)

Premenstrual dysphoric disorder can be viewed as the amplification of premenstrual syndrome (PMS) and is an intense and persistent mood disorder that occurs a week or two before the period starts.

It can affect a woman's physical and emotional well-being, exhibiting any of these varied symptoms in different individuals:

- Anxiety
- Irritability and intense mood swings
- Food cravings
- Bloating
- Fatigue

- Difficulty concentrating
- Breast tenderness
- Irregular sleep patterns
- Feelings of sadness or unrest

The causes of PMDD are considered to be a combination of genetic and environmental factors and hormonal imbalances. Some women are more genetically inclined to suffer from PMDD and are, therefore, more likely to feel its effects. Similarly, distressing circumstances like poor sleep and stress may trigger the disorder. Lastly, changes in hormones like estrogen and progesterone in the days up to a woman's period can influence her mood and, therefore, her behavior.

5. Bipolar disorder (BD)

Bipolar disorder, formerly known as manic depression, is a mental condition that manifests in extreme mood, energy, and behavior shifts. It occurs in episodes of high energy 'up' moods (mania) and low depressive states.

In the mania phase, a person may experience increased energy, a buzzing mind, and feelings of elation and grandeur. In the depressive episodes, they are likely to experience the symptoms of major depression, including emotions like sadness, inadequacy, and despair, and depleted energy levels.

BD is chronic and recurring, and the episodes come and go over time. Like other forms of depression, the causes of bipolar disorder are considered a combination of biological, environmental, and psychological factors.

A BD diagnosis can be difficult to come to terms with. Research indicates that suicide rates among BD patients are 10-30 times higher than the general population. Moreover, up to 20% of people with BD end their life by suicide, especially when it goes untreated (Dome et al., 2019).

Yet it can also be liberating to understand why you go through the seemingly uncontrollable shifts. Former Disney star and actress Selena Gomez was diagnosed with BD in 2018. In an interview with Elle magazine, she confessed that she was relieved at the news, *"I felt a huge weight lifted off me when I found out. I could take a deep breath and go, 'Okay, that explains so much.'"* (Chocano, 2021)

6. Seasonal Affective Disorder (SAD)

Seasonal Affective Disorder is a form of major depression that shifts as the seasons change. It develops in the fall and builds through winter when there are shorter days and lower exposure to sunlight. Similarly, it goes away as the days get longer in the spring and summer.

The symptoms of SAD include:

- Changes in appetite and weight
- Irritability
- Social withdrawal
- Low energy
- Trouble concentrating on tasks
- Sleep irregularities
- Feelings of hopelessness

The potential causes of SAD are a mix of biological, environmental, and psychological factors. These elements include changes in the circadian rhythm, light sensitivity, and brain serotonin level shifts. Light therapy can help manage SAD and involves exposure to a specialized light box with higher light intensity than regular lighting.

7. Situational Depression

Situational depression differs from other forms of depression in that it is triggered by a specific event rather than as a continual problem. Distressing events like the death of a loved one, loss of a job, financial instability, or a medical diagnosis can trigger situational depression. Changing jobs or moving to a new city or country could also trigger situational depression.

A person experiencing situational depression will experience symptoms similar to major depression and other types of depression, including loss of interest in previously enjoyed activities, fatigue, low energy levels, and sleep and appetite irregularities. They battle with feelings of worthlessness, anxiety, sadness, loneliness, and suicidal thoughts.

8. Psychotic Depression

Psychotic depression is a form of major depression that exhibits psychotic features. It is also known as 'major depressive disorder with psychotic features' and displays the symptoms of depression along with psychotic aspects like:

- Delusions
- Hallucinations
- Paranoia
- Disorganized thinking

A person with psychotic depression will also experience depressive symptoms similar to major depression. They lose their enthusiasm for work and pleasurable activities, have low energy, and have feelings of despair and guilt. Moreover, they may have muddled speech and odd behavior.

Psychotic depression can be mistaken for other mental disorders and is difficult to diagnose. Lack of proper diagnosis and treatment is dangerous, as it disrupts the quality of daily life and could prompt suicidal thoughts.

9. Atypical depression

Atypical depression can easily be mistaken as it portrays symptoms not usually present with other types of depression. A person with atypical depression may find themselves overeating, oversleeping, and having heightened sensitivity to rejection and criticism. They also experience temporarily increased mood levels when something good happens.

Atypical depression is more likely to affect patients with bipolar disorder as they experience mood, energy, and behavior shifts between the manic and depressive episodes. Other manifestations of atypical depression will include the usual symptoms of depression, such as heightened anxiety, increased sadness, low self-esteem, heavy fatigue, and trouble concentrating. The person may feel easily overwhelmed and have difficulty making decisions.

Atypical depression is believed to be prompted by genetic factors, medical conditions, and stressful life events.

The Cognitive-Behavioral View of Depression

Negative thoughts fuel depression. Though we all experience automatic negative thoughts, a person with depression will likely live with a constant stream of statements like-

> *"I'm not good at anything."*
>
> *"I will never be happy."*
>
> *"I am the worst person to the people around me."*

Some of the thoughts that Jessi from Big Mouth had included,

> *"My dad will have a baby with another woman and forget all about me."*
>
> *"We will never be a happy family again."*

Depressive thoughts can be irrational and often stem from underlying cognitive distortions. A polarized perspective may trigger self-defeat with reactions like, "My boss shouted at me today. I must be a horrible employee."

Similarly, mind reading is a reasonably common distortion when battling depression, making conclusions about people and events without supporting evidence. Lucy might think Jared dislikes her because he ignored her in the break room. Sometimes mind reading persists even where there is contrary evidence, so Jared could engage Lucy in a fun conversation yet still leave her thinking, *"He is only talking to me to be nice, not because he likes me or finds me interesting."*

Jessi in Big Mouth blames herself for the problems with her parents. She believes that they were happy until she came along. Self-blaming can be prominent with thoughts like,

> *"I ruin everything I touch."*
>
> *"Maybe this presentation would have been better if I wasn't part of it."*

These thoughts are likely to affect a person's sense of self-worth and esteem and contribute to feelings of hopelessness.

As a result, they may isolate themselves from friends and, even where they want to be part of a community, feel that they **should** be a particular type of way to be acceptable. The person will struggle to get through activities they previously enjoyed, perhaps prompted by thoughts like, "I'm not good at this anyway."

Jessi's cognitive behavioral cycle was something like this:

Trigger/ situation:
Parents getting a divorce and moving on with other people

Thoughts:
It's my fault that my parents are separating.
If I weren't born, my parents would still be happy.

Feelings:
Extended sadness, neglect, self-hatred

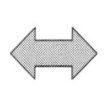

⟷

Behavior:
Skipping classes
Acting out and lashing out at her parents
Trying out drugs

CBT interventions work to question the irrational thoughts and underlying core beliefs about ourselves and others that drive the depressive motions. During therapy, Jessi and her therapist would work through her thoughts about her parents' separation, digging through the perceptions of these events. With evidence supporting the idea that her parents' failing relationship is separate from her and does not diminish their love for her, perhaps she could see life a bit more like this:

Trigger/ situation:
Parents getting a divorce and moving on with other people

Thoughts:
My parents' separation is not my fault. Whatever happens with them, they still love me.

Feelings:
Sadness but acceptance

Behavior:
Hanging out with her friends again

Helping her dad move into the new house

Knowledge is the first step to healing and change. When embarking on a wellness journey, it helps to know the magnitude of the iceberg. This chapter explored anxiety and depression and their breadths.

Anxiety and depression can weigh heavily on the mind, even where they are unnoticed. When left untreated, these disorders deteriorate our mental and physical health. Medication and therapy can go a long way in breaking the repetitive negative thinking patterns. In the next chapter, we will consider CBT interventions that can help manage these disorders and how best to practice consistently.

CBT Techniques for Anxiety and Depression

No storm, not even the one in your life, can last forever. The storm is just passing over.

-Iyanla Vanzant (2001)

Cognitive behavioral therapy demonstrates effectiveness in managing multiple anxiety and depression disorders, including panic disorder, obsessive-compulsive disorder, major depressive disorder, persistent depressive disorder, bipolar disorder, specific phobias, and more.

This chapter delves into the techniques to improve our mood and approach to situations. CBT tools anchor heavily on becoming aware of negative thoughts as they happen and challenging these thoughts to allow replacement. Cognitive restructuring tools like journaling and thought lists come in handy to build awareness, while Socratic questioning and putting thoughts on trial offer challenging room. Activity scheduling helps boost our mood by injecting us with the thrill of accomplishing tasks. That and relaxation techniques are great for overcoming depressive sessions and anxious undercurrents.

Cognitive Restructuring

The interconnectedness of our thoughts, emotions, and behavior, and their capacity to influence one another, can have devastating consequences when out of balance. Negative thoughts will stimulate negative emotions causing unhelpful behavior. Likewise, negative behavior reinforces negative thoughts and feelings, growing into chronic disorders like depression.

This very loop presents the key to transformation. If our thoughts shape how we feel and act, then changing these thoughts can change our emotions and actions.

In Chapter 2, we discussed the steps of a CBT program. Cognitive behavioral therapy aims to alter our overall well-being by improving our thoughts and subsequent emotions and behavior about a situation.

Many techniques employ cognitive restructuring to identify and criticize negative and irrational thoughts and the distortions driving these thoughts. Cognitive restructuring is a process that combines multiple approaches to challenge negative thoughts and ultimately form new, positive thinking patterns.

Identifying negative thoughts/ cognitive distortions

Awareness is the first step towards change. As we realized in the previous chapters, automatic thoughts often happen so quickly and silently that they are unnoticeable. We may be able to tell that we feel afraid, sad, or hopeless but remain oblivious to the thoughts beyond these feelings.

CBT begins with catching these irrational thoughts and takes practice. The tools work from the known to the unknown, starting with surface-level behavior and emotions. Looking at the symptoms of sadness, rage, or worry and highlighting unhelpful behavior requiring work makes it easier to zoom in on the distortions that led to the spiral.

Journaling is a helpful tool for examining these patterns and recording experiences along with the surrounding thoughts, emotions, and behavior.

Journaling towards Clarity

Journaling can be an enormously effective tool for mental health improvement. The mind stores a lot of information and constantly processes new data, so some details could easily slip through the cracks. You may remember what you wore to the meeting last month, your presentation, and even your coffee, but forget what song was playing on the radio in the cab.

Journaling presents a means to retain as much detail as possible about a situation. In the Harry Potter series, Professor Dumbledore shows Harry his pensieve, a shallow stone basin with which he collects and views memories.

The magical basin helped the headmaster ease the swirling thoughts in his mind by holding those he stored safely and allowing him to revisit places and events repeatedly.

Dumbledore tells Harry, *"One simply siphons the excess thoughts from one's mind, pours them into the basin, and examines them at leisure. It becomes easier to spot patterns and links, you understand, when they are in this form."* (Rowling, 2000)

The pensieve also allowed him to take Harry along on these journeys, and together they filled vital knowledge gaps that would later help Harry defeat the dark wizard, Lord Voldemort (Rowling, 2005).

Though it may not possess magical or supernatural qualities, journaling is like the carved stone bowl in many ways. It helps organize chaotic thoughts and discern feelings. The input can help identify patterns, thereby drawing out variables that may have been previously unnoticed. Moreover, returning to the entries is valuable when measuring progress, say, the days you worked out or the gradual diet adjustment.

Journaling is sometimes considered a complex activity demanding entries along the lines of the famous Shakespearean quote, *'In sooth I know not why I am sad'* (Shakespeare, 2017). Yet it need not be. Some people write poetry and metaphors, trying to interpret what runs in their minds. Others prefer to go straight to the point and use as few words as possible. Some don't even like the idea of pen and paper.

There are many ways to journal, with no right or wrong. Speaking of pen and paper, common journaling alternatives to the traditional diary include:

- Smartphone apps
- Computer apps like word-doc or Google Docs
- Recording thoughts as an audio journal
- Video journals by recording yourself, your surroundings or both
- Using visual journals that focus more on images than words, like an art journal

Whatever the preferred journaling form, keeping an information log helps to clarify previously obscure issues and keep track of goals.

The benefits of keeping a journal include:

- It helps to ease anxiety by expressing the fear and allowing yourself to work through it
- It is valuable for depression and other mood disorders by helping to identify NATs and cognitive distortions
- It helps with stress management, allowing you to calm down as you let out the stressors
- It improves clarity and boosts problem-solving capacity
- It aids healthy habit development by keeping track of current emotions, thoughts, and behavior and identifying negative patterns. Journaling then records
- new actions, eventual habits, and emotional and mental changes.
- It helps with goal setting by exploring positive elements like values and authentic desires.

ACTIVITY

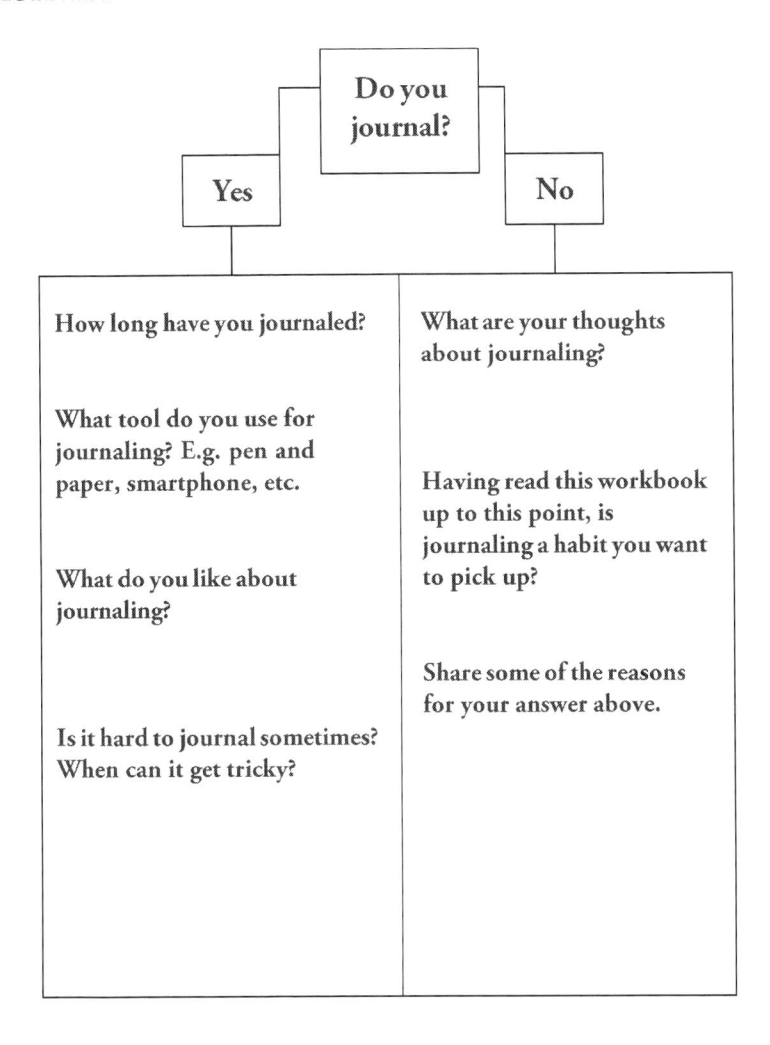

```
        ┌─────────────┐
        │  Do you     │
        │  journal?   │
        └─────────────┘
        ╱             ╲
  ┌─────┐             ┌─────┐
  │ Yes │             │ No  │
  └─────┘             └─────┘
```

Yes	**No**
How long have you journaled?	What are your thoughts about journaling?
What tool do you use for journaling? E.g. pen and paper, smartphone, etc.	Having read this workbook up to this point, is journaling a habit you want to pick up?
What do you like about journaling?	Share some of the reasons for your answer above.
Is it hard to journal sometimes? When can it get tricky?	

Tips when Journaling for Anxiety

Anxiety sends the mind into overdrive, brooding over thoughts that spur fear or worry. Journaling can help remove these thoughts from the mind and put them before you for objective assessment.

Here are a few reminders when going through a bout of anxiety:

I. It is okay to journal wherever you are, whenever you need to

Anxiety can be inconvenient, striking at the most random time or place. A small notebook or smartphone app can be handy whenever such situations arise.

II. Review what you write often, looking for patterns

Journaling is a gift for your present and future self. At present, it allows you to let out the worrying thoughts about a situation for review. In the future, it will be a source of information that can help identify similar elements in different situations triggering anxiety, reactive behavior, progressive improvement, etc.

Make it a habit to review your journals occasionally, especially when tracking your progress with a goal.

III. Use the writing to keep you in control

When in a threatening situation (real or imagined), the spiraling thoughts continue to breed fear and worry in a distressing cycle. Journaling can help break this cycle when you list the thoughts making you anxious and then use evidence to challenge them successively. Moreover, journaling can help you focus on the things within your control and work on these to regain calm.

Tips when Journaling for Depression

When dealing with depression, it can be challenging to see past the dark cloud. Keeping a journal can be a valuable catalyst to breaking through the clouds by helping you shift focus. Thinking through your values and the things that give life meaning and exploring them through a daily catalog can help rekindle a joyful flame.

Here are a few pointers when journaling amid depression

I. Allow yourself to start small

Journaling can feel like a lot of pressure, especially when running on low energy. So, make it as least pressure as possible. Plan a time to journal and make it a simple exercise you can build on. For example, schedule about ten minutes when you wake up or before bed to jot down a few thoughts.

II. Write beyond the negative things

Writing can often be an intense, cathartic process that digs deep into the mind and soul. As such, it becomes easier to express the painful parts of our lives when we have gotten used to journaling. However, with too much focus on the negative than the positive, we can get carried away on wave after wave of despair and melancholy.

So, it helps to input positive aspects of daily life too. When there are entries about the day you woke up early and caught the sunrise, the drive you went on with your friend that was a rush of exhilaration, the fantastic cup of coffee and warm croissant at the cafe…

these seemingly small events become potent sources of good energy and motivation to work through things and grow.

III. Use prompts where getting started falters

Take a hand where you need it. If getting started is difficult, think of leading questions or statements that point you in an opening direction.

Consider the box below for simple prompts that can help kickstart a journaling session on a hard day.

Simple Journaling Prompts

1. Think about your day ahead (or the day you had). What activities did you have, and how did you feel about them (or what actions do you have planned and how do you feel about them)?
2. How did you wake up feeling?
3. Write about the feelings/ emotions you experience.
    a. Write three things you are grateful for today
    b. Write five things that made you happy this week
    c. Write three things that make you feel anxious or upset
4. Write letters
    a. Write a letter to someone that has hurt you/ yourself, saying what you could not tell them.
    b. Write a letter to your past self-acknowledging their effort to get you where you are now.
    c. Write a letter to your future self-describing what you are hopeful for and the changes you look forward to making.

5. Write out your strengths and how they have come to your aid in previous situations. Think about how they can help you overcome a present challenge.

6. Make a list of things you can control and cannot control but can accept (about five each).

ACTIVITY

Keeping a journal is one of the most effective CBT tools because it helps us gain deeper insight into ourselves. Thought logs allow one to input as much information about a situation as possible.

For the next week, schedule time to journal intentionally. The best times are in the morning before the day begins or in the evening when winding down the day. You do not have to spend too long or overthink the daily entries. Instead, use each session as an opportunity to sort through the mess and bring it out coherently.

Consider this thought log structure for your journal entries as you begin the work to reshape how you react to situations. The input does not have to be arranged in a table as below (say if you already have a journal) and could be in prose as long as it captures these central aspects of our cognitive-behavioral process.

Trigger	Thoughts	Emotions	Behavior	Alternative thought
'… this happened today.'	'I immediately found myself thinking….' 'My mind automatically went to….'	'I felt…'	'I did…' 'I said…'	'In hindsight, I could have done/said…'
Illustration:				
My husband snapped at me this morning. He wouldn't explain what was wrong when I asked and left for work seemingly angry.'	I must have done something to offend him. We've been distant lately. Maybe he is not attracted to me anymore.	Sad Undesirable	Was irritable and distracted at work. Made a few silly errors in my report and yelled at the intern for pointing them out.	I'm not sure what I did to offend my husband. We did not have a fight or disagreement. Maybe he is having a bad morning and is only transferring it. I should take a few minutes to calm down and let it go before work.'

Day 1	Day 2	Day 3	Day 4	Day 5

Entry Instructions

Element	Instructions	Illustration
Trigger	Elaborate on the event that led to unfavorable emotions or behavior. Record the facts without making assumptions or illustrations.	In the evening, I saw a group of youngsters ahead on my path to the store.
Thoughts	Thoughts tend to happen in a monologue or conversation fashion. Allow yourself the freedom of expression and use statements and questions as they occur.	What if they attack me and steal my bag? Am I safe? I should not have been outside so late.
Emotions	Use a word or phrase to describe how you felt. Sometimes emotions move like a wave. Indicate this process where it occurred.	Anxious
Behavior	Input what you did or how you reacted to the situation.	I turned back and increased my pace to a near-run. I didn't even stop at the grocery store to get what I needed.
Alternate thought	Looking back on the situation, what different views could you have had?	Maybe they are just a bunch of young people enjoying their evening. I ought to be cautious but don't have to stop attending to my business and run back home.

ACTIVITY

Random-thought List

It helps to identify the variations in which a cognitive distortion occurs as we observe the comings and goings of our thoughts. An event like butchering a presentation could spur many thoughts, and catching as many as possible increases the scope of personal awareness.

The mind race track, in this case, might look something like this:

> *'They should have picked someone else to make the presentation.'*
>
> *'I make terrible presentations.'*
>
> *'I bet I'll get a negative appraisal or a downward review.'*
>
> *'Why can't I be good at anything?'*
>
> *'They must think I am unqualified for the job.'*
>
> *'Maybe I am unqualified for the job.'*
>
> *"I should have done better.'*

While thinking through each day's entry, consider the thoughts flitting through the mind at each event. What occurred to you..? What did you think about yourself and your surroundings? What random forms did the views take? How many variations of the thoughts did you experience?

Consider how you felt if you cannot immediately place the thoughts. Were you sad? What made you sad? What else made you sad? Dig around every emotion for the underlying thoughts and note them below.

Day 1: What was the emotion?   Random thought variations
Day 2: What was the emotion?   Random thought variations
Day 3: What was the emotion?   Random thought variations
Day 4: What was the emotion?   Random thought variations

> **Day 5:**
>
> What was the emotion?
>
> Random thought variations

Examining core beliefs

Core beliefs are the deeply held assumptions about ourselves, others, and the world. Our beliefs shape how we think, perceive reality, and behave. Core beliefs often stem from childhood and our socialization into adulthood.

Core beliefs are often not based on facts. However, the power of attraction draws evidence that reinforces what we believe. Core beliefs can be difficult to change and require digging past cognitive distortions.

For example, if I believe that I am unworthy of love, I will tend to find myself experiencing the lack of love in different situations and affirming the idea. Even when I encounter genuine love, I may believe it is a hoax or ruse for selfish gain.

ACTIVITY

1. How do you view the world around you?
Complete the statements below. Refrain from lingering or overthinking. Simply note what first comes to mind.

I am

_____

Other people are

_____

The world is

_____

2. How do the impulsive beliefs make you feel?
Consider the answers above. When do you recall becoming aware of these strong opinions about yourself and others? What life experiences have built up these beliefs? Does anyone around you hold the same ideas?

How do you feel about what you believe?

_____

_____

_____

_____

_____

3. Are these beliefs helpful?

Are the beliefs constructive? Do they build up into healthy thoughts? If not, what thoughts about yourself, others, and the world do you suppose would be more life-giving? Note the beliefs you would like to nurture.

I am

_____

Other people are

_____

The world is

_____

4. How would the new beliefs be helpful in practice?

Pick a previously recorded event where you did not like what you thought, felt, or did.

How would the new beliefs change how you perceive the same or a similar situation? What would be different?

_____
_____
_____
_____

Challenging negative distortions

Cognitive distortions provide a skewed lens through which to perceive events. A person prone to catastrophizing will see the worst possible outcome from a minor event and rack up anxiety that was perhaps unnecessary. When we can question the validity of these thoughts, we allow ourselves the idea that our deep-rooted convictions are not as accurate as they seem.

Tools that help challenge negative thoughts include Socratic questioning, decatastrophizing, and taking thoughts to court.

Socratic Questioning

Socrates believed that using structured questions to teach allowed the teacher to assume the back seat and the student to take the knowledge wheel. Deep questions focusing on underlying concepts, principles, and theories led the scholars to uncover and reexamine ideas reaching for the truth.

The philosopher's teaching model has widespread application today, with teachers and students engaging in a conversation that allows thought probing. Socratic questioning in psychotherapy helps evaluate an idea by asking systematic questions that dig into the underlying distortions using structured logic.

ACTIVITY

1. Questions provide the basis for challenging identified cognitive distortions.

Pick an irrational thought that occurred to you in a distressing situation.

Note it below.

_____

_____

_____

Now, subject the thought to some or all of the questions below, taking a few minutes to think about each answer. Give each question adequate time, being as objective as possible.

1. Does my thought anchor on facts or feelings?
   Facts are undeniable evidence. Feelings, though significant, can be flighty.
2. What is the evidence supporting this thought?
3. Am I jumping to conclusions or making assumptions based on too little data?
4. Is my current view the only way to look at it?
5. What are the benefits and problems of thinking this way?
6. Is this thought born out of habit or verifiable data?
7. Am I expecting myself to be perfect?

8. Am I making things about me even when they have little or nothing to do with me on a personal level?
9. Am I applying a double standard?
10. Am I assuming that there is no way to change the situation?

What are some of the answers to the above questions? Do they help realize the irrational assumptions and distortions? Share the observations below.

_____

_____

_____

_____

Decatastrophizing

When we experience a flurry of emotions in an anxious or depressed state, we tend to assume the worst. Decatastrophizing examines how exaggerated these assumptions are by asking, what is the worst that could happen? What is the worst-case scenario?

The activity involves digging into each worst-case scenario, breaking the floor beneath every assumption until the worst possible outcome is reached. At this point, it begins to occur to us that perhaps what we feared so greatly is not as bad as initially imagined.

ACTIVITY

Think about an event that makes you anxious or depressed. It could be an upcoming presentation or social gathering. It could be a thing that happens habitually, and that fuels the extended feelings of worry, dread, or despair.

What thoughts do you have about this event?

_____

_____

_____

_____

_____

What if what you thought happened? What could be the worst outcome of things not going well?

_____

_____

What would be the consequences of that outcome? What is the worst thing about those consequences happening?

_____

_____

What will be the most terrible thing at this point? What if what you worry about here happens? What is the worst?

How do you feel about the situation now? Is the worst of the worst perceivable outcome as terrifying as it was before? Is it as catastrophic as you initially thought or felt?

Taking Thoughts to Court

When taking thoughts to court, you play the roles of a defense lawyer, prosecutor, and judge. We tend to believe our thoughts and feelings about a situation, especially when using emotional reasoning. Putting these thoughts on trial is a great way to challenge them without diminishing our sense of self and our feelings about our ability to reason.

As the defense lawyer, you present the evidence supporting the thought. Why is it valid? What is it based on?

The prosecutor will then present material against the thought to disprove its validity. Where is the flaw in the defense's argument?

Like a legal court, only valid and verifiable facts are admissible. Opinions and assumptions do not hold as they are sentiments rather than actual data.

Finally, as the judge, you will weigh both sides and the multiple perspectives arriving at a verdict on the fairness and accuracy of the thought.

Role-play Activity

Assume these roles and fill in the fields below.

The defendant

Pick out another thought from when you were anxious or depressed. What went through your mind on that occasion?

Present the thought to the court.

The defense argument	The prosecution
Present the facts supporting this thought. Take time to gather the evidence, reviewing the situation from multiple angles as you would for an actual defendant. Leave every possible, verifiable argument on the floor.	Present the case against the thought. Again, time to gather the evidence, reviewing the situation from multiple angles as you would against an actual defendant. Leave every possible, verifiable argument on the floor.

The judge's verdict

Weigh the defense vs the prosecution.

What argument holds more water? Is the thought justifiable, accurate, and fair?

Declare a verdict against the thought.

1. Activity Scheduling

Activity scheduling is a therapeutic tool that proposes repeatedly engaging in enjoyable activities to help improve mood and eventual well-being. Activity scheduling, also called behavioral activation (BA), focuses on changing behavior to change thoughts and emotions.

People in a depressive phase tend to isolate themselves from their friends and family. As the zeal for engaging in previously enjoyed activities dwindles, it takes the desire to interact with other humans, breeding thoughts like how unpleasant their company would be. Yet isolation further fuels low feelings like sadness at being left out, lower self-esteem from the belief of being unwanted, etc.

Research indicates that intentionally planning and going through with activities and social engagements increases positive assurance and self-support. A study on older primary care patients in care management for depression found positive associations between activity scheduling, self-reported engagement, and depression over 12 months (Riebe et al., 2012).

Planning an activity gives us something to look forward to and can help elevate moods, just as we got excited about the trip to the zoo on our birthday and waited for it for weeks.

Activity scheduling is straightforward but requires overcoming some of the most challenging hurdles- getting up and out. Though having friends invite us over reinforces the awareness that we are loved and cared for no matter what we are going through, taking the step to reach out and plan the activity is a stronger reinforcement when working through depression or getting out of a funk. Self-initiation cements the knowledge that there is more beyond the dark cloud, and we can go out there for it.

The best place to start is by identifying your values and finding related enjoyable activities. Meaningful values that are sources of pleasant activities include:

- Physical fitness- exercise, walks, hikes, etc
- Participating in hobbies- learning a new language, practicing an instrument, etc
- Nurturing relationships- planning dates with friends and loved ones, scheduling phone calls, etc
- Self-education- taking up a new course, learning a new skill, etc
- Self-care- making time for meditation, yoga, weekends off, etc

ACTIVITY

a. Do you know your personal values? Rate the comments below to find out what areas you relate with the most (especially on the 'good' days), which could become intentionally scheduled activities. Use a scale of 1-5 to rate your response, with one being poor and five being excellent.

Comments	1	2	3	4	5
a. I enjoy taking walks					
b. I invest in the fun things I like, e.g. buying art supplies.					
c. My friends are a great source of comfort.					
d. I would like to extend my list of skills.					
e. I make time for myself.					
a. I feel a sense of freedom in the great outdoors.					
b. I find myself creative and artistic.					

c.	Family is important to me.				
d.	I like to cosy up with a good book.				
e.	A quiet, meditative space is soothing.				
a.	I channel my frustration into physical exertion like running or punching a bag.				
b.	I play/ have always wanted to play an instrument.				
c.	I make time for people when they need someone to talk to.				
d.	I listen to podcasts or read articles often.				
e.	I am mindful of the energy I take in and let out.				
a.	Sports are a thrilling activity.				
b.	I can spend hours working on a fun, recreational project.				
c.	The world is less scary when I know I have people I can count on.				
d.	I could spend hours online learning something new.				
e.	I try to make time for relaxing activities like weekend trips or yoga retreats.				

Key
a. Physical fitness enthusiast
b. Excited about hobbies
c. Relationship oriented
d. Big on self-education
e. Self-care champion

How did you score?

What letters had 3-5 ratings? These few checkers indicate the qualities that are meaningful in your life.

_____

_____

_____

_____

b. Now, intentionally schedule activities for the next four weeks based on the most substantial values above. (Consider activities you have been avoiding or would want to avoid out of disinterest or heightened anxiety.)

The activities could be once per week for a start and to allow for the busyness of life.

Fill in the table below over the four weeks, being intentional with the timings.

What activity did you schedule?	When did you schedule the activity for?	What did you think and feel after scheduling the activity?	What did you think and feel after completing the activity?
Week 1:			
Week 2:			

Week 3:			
Week 4:			

2. Relaxation Techniques

Breathing is essential for life as it is for emotional, mental, and spiritual balance. Techniques like yoga and meditation incorporate the power of the breath to build mental strength and focus.

Intentional breathwork involves the lungs, diaphragm, and intercostal muscles and is a fantastic mental health tool because it is freely and readily available. Though seemingly simple, breathwork provides a myriad of benefits with consistent practice.

Breathing exercises decrease stress and anxiety and help with relaxation. As we take long, slow inhales and exhales, the nervous system shifts from sympathetic to parasympathetic function, helping to get out of fight-or-flight mode. Consequential muscle relaxation helps ease tension, improve sleep and rest, and boost cognitive and physical health.

Moreover, physical health components like movement become easier with breathwork. As the lungs exercise their holding capacity, running up the stairs or jumping rope becomes less strenuous and more enjoyable. Moreover, breathing techniques ease complications like asthma and chronic obstructive pulmonary disease (COPD) (Srivastava et al., 2005)

3. Breathing Techniques and Exercises

Deep relaxation breathing

Deep relaxation breathing involves expanding the diaphragm by inhaling deeply and following through with a slow exhale. Also called abdominal, relaxation, or diaphragmatic breathing, DRB uses deep, slow, even breaths that expand the stomach, unlike shallow breathing, where only the chest moves when inhaling and exhaling.

Progressive muscle relaxation

Progressive muscle relaxation involves creating tension by actively contracting the muscles and then sequentially releasing them throughout the body. PMR can quickly help ease anxiety and is a good technique for managing a panic attack.

The 5-4-3-2-1 exercise

A panic attack can come with a lightheadedness that feels mildly dispositioning. The 5-4-3-2-1 exercise brings you back to solid ground through the five senses. It involves looking at five things (sight), listening to four sounds (hearing), touching three objects (touch), picking out two essences (smell), and identifying one thing you can taste.

> **Additional Calming Tips**
>
> 1. Even when experiencing heavy motions, remember that feelings and situations are temporary. The tide will change. Allow that to help reshape the thoughts you hold about the future.
>
> 2. Practice looking at thoughts and situations from different perspectives. There are often multiple ways to look at a situation. Remember the Socratic questioning process and employ it even in minor cases to build a self-evaluation habit.

3. Along with assessing thoughts and situations from multiple perspectives, practice exploring diverse solutions to a problem. Creative solutions build the capacity to handle more triggers using a portfolio of options.

4. It is honorable to take responsibility for a mistake. However, blaming is not always necessary and only aggravates the situation.

5. Practice gratitude for the small and big things. The energy of gratitude will remind you of simple joys and may carry you through a dark day.

6. You are not alone. Millions of people are going through what you are going through. Breathe. Remember that you are human.

CBT techniques are practical and fact-driven. These interventions build mental resilience against disorders like anxiety and depression by challenging our negative thoughts and beliefs.

In this chapter, we explored the numerous tools that can help restructure our outlook and manage the fear-based and despair-based symptoms of anxiety and depression. In the next chapter, we will work on a few techniques that aid in stress management

CBT for Stress Management

What worries you, masters you.

- John Locke (1690)

As the previous chapter shows, anxiety and depression sometimes inhibit productivity and disrupt normal functioning like rest, sleep, and feeding patterns. These changes influence our well-being and promote unhealthy effects like stress.

American philosopher and psychologist William James intimated that the greatest weapon against stress is our ability to choose one thought over another (n.d.). In a similar vein, Hans Seyle(1956), in his work studying the hypothetical, non-specific response of an organism to stressors, suggested that it is not stress that kills us but our reaction to it.

This chapter will examine the types of stress we experience and the manifesting symptoms. We will consider that not all stress is bad: In fact, studies show that positive stress, also called 'eustress', plays a role in boosting cognitive performance, memory, and overall health. We will then look at the causes of chronic stress, which lies on the detrimental end of the spectrum. Finally, we shall embark on CBT techniques to help manage stress better.

Contemplate Pete below, who has been in a stressful situation for months:

> Pete glances at the phone ringing and feels the familiar pulse quickening. It is the landlord again calling about rent. This is the second time she has called this month, and she has recently taken to calling every month.
>
> Pete considers ignoring the call but knows that it will hardly help. Besides, he's not refusing to pay rent- he just hasn't been paid in months. Last month, Pete explained his situation to the impatient woman. Towards the end of last year, he had two clients who owed him a pretty sum of money for his services. But almost as though they had discussed it, they both suddenly declared that they could not pay him due to the post-COVID recession and force-stopped the gigs. It has been five months since then, and not a penny owed has arrived at his bank.
>
> Pete had to start again with new clients but still needs to submit more work to get steady pay. In the last few months, he has had to beg and borrow from all his friends to get by and pay part of the rent. Some were very understanding and loaned him some cash without a specific payback date. Others made snide comments about his unstable job and how he has been in this position for years.

Pete worries daily about how he will afford dinner and constantly takes up more jobs than he can handle to meet the deficit. However, the anxiety and stress have affected his creativity and productivity, and he is constantly late with the deliverables. His cable was disconnected two months ago after failing to keep up with the monthly payments. He last bought a new pair of shoes a few years ago, and his old ones are steadily getting worn out.

Pete recently started avoiding family functions. He does not like the comments about his weight loss and the fatigue on his face. He hates making himself laugh at the uncomfortable comments and pretending that all is well.

He drinks and smokes on the weekend to relieve the pressure of getting through each day. Recently, he has upped his intake from a few shots of cheap vodka to a bottle by sundown on Sunday. He is not sleeping well and sometimes feels quite overwhelmed on Mondays.

He picks up the phone with a heavy sigh and listens to the woman on the other end of the line, intermittently saying 'yes', 'I understand', and 'I am sorry, I am doing my best'. After a few minutes, he hangs up, puts the phone aside and lays his head on his desk.

Stress at a Hormonal Level

We often perceive stress as bad, but it is essentially a signal. When we detect a real or imagined threat, such as narrowly avoiding an accident, a small part of the brain called the hypothalamus initiates the stress response. This stress response sends signals to the adrenal glands as the body releases hormones to help gear up for fight-or-flight.

The main stress hormones are cortisol and adrenaline. Cortisol increases glucose in the bloodstream, stimulating the brain and muscle repair functions. Cortisol also helps the body to build efficiency by inhibiting non-essential functions like digestive and reproductive systems.

Adrenaline works with cortisol by aiding the muscles to utilize the increased glucose in the bloodstream.

The body's response to stress is not necessarily a harmful thing. Exposure to short-term stress has shown positive effects like increased cognitive functioning and memory. However, the prolonged release of stress hormones and the resulting responses negatively impact the body in the long run.

The Types of Stress

1. Acute stress

Acute stress is short-term and arises as the body reacts to a new or testing situation like an upcoming presentation, a strict work deadline, or escaping a dangerous event. Acute stress may also occur due to an enjoyable, thrilling event like a rollercoaster ride. The effects of acute stress tend to be temporary, and the mental, physical and emotional states return to normal within a short while.

Exercises like mindfulness and breathing techniques can help to ease the distress and talk yourself through the stress.

The symptoms of acute stress include:

- Increased heart rate occurs as part of the fight-or-flight response
- Pupil dilation allows more light into the eyes for better sight
- Rapid and heavy breathing lets more oxygen into the respiratory system for a more efficient reaction to the stress
- Feelings of worry or fear (accelerated anxiety)
- Perspiration as the body temperature rises and causes sweating
- Irritability and mood swings as the internal balance shifts
- Erratic sleep as a result of the upheaval

2. Episodic acute stress

Episodic acute stress occurs when acute pressures are frequent such as repeated intense presentations or continuous pressing work deadlines. The challenge is that the body does not get enough time to reset between the stressors. Moreover, we sometimes drift towards unhealthy coping mechanisms like overdrinking and prolonged drug use, further aggravating episodic acute stress's effects.

Unmanaged episodic acute stress can bring about damaging challenges such as hypertension. While it may be difficult to eliminate the stress trigger, such as a large, rigidly-timed project in a lump sum, small steps towards the big goal can help to manage the stress.

In this case, consider working on the project in small portions every day or leveraging collaborative strategies.

The symptoms of episodic acute stress include:

- Feeling overwhelmed- frequent episodes of your boss shouting your ear off about the work that is due and your slacking may provoke the feeling of being overwhelmed and unable to keep up with the challenges.
- Muscle tension- our muscles get tense when we undergo stress but relax after the situation has passed. Without adequate resting time, muscle tension builds up
- Migraines- these are often caused by muscle tension. Migraines may become more frequent and intense as the episodic acute stress accelerates.
- Shorter leash on anger and irritability- as stress breeds, it becomes increasingly difficult to brush over things that were previously easier to overlook.

3. Chronic stress

Chronic stress sets in when stressors have continued unmanaged for an extended period up to years. The triggers for this kind of stress are often beyond our control and therefore carry a heavy sense of powerlessness, such as a chronic illness, poverty, or war. Additionally, a person who experienced a traumatic childhood may view life through a chronically stressed lens even if the present circumstances seem fine.

Sometimes, the triggers are more driven by the mindset than by actual circumstances. Perhaps because chronic stress lurks around for so long that it is almost a regular part of one's life, the efforts to overcome it tend to wane over time.

If chronic stress goes untreated, it can have detrimental health effects such as depression and heart disease.

The symptoms of chronic stress include:

- Insomnia- erratic sleep patterns develop into challenges falling and staying asleep and getting enough rest
- Chronic headaches- tension migraines become part of normal programming, occurring as often as 15 days a month (D'Amico et al., 2000)
- Panic attacks- the feelings of fear and worry graduate into panic attacks triggered by the symptoms of acute stress
- Unhealthy feeding patterns and weight gain- Some people 'stress eat' and binge on unhealthy foods like junk. Weight gain can also result from hormonal imbalances due to the prolonged release of stress hormones.
- Fatigue- carrying our distressed emotions around is more exhausting than we think. As chronic stress persists, so does the feeling of fatigue, regardless of the hours of sleep or rest.

Other symptoms of unaddressed stress include:

- Abnormal heartbeat (arrhythmia)
- Asthma outbreaks
- Changes in sex drive
- Hardening of the arteries (atherosclerosis)
- Heartburn, ulcers, or irritable bowel syndrome
- High blood pressure
- Stomach upsets- constipation, cramps, diarrhea
- Skin problems such as acne or eczema

8 Potential Benefits of Short-Term Stress

Psychologists identify positive stress, which helps you stay alert and energized to endure testing situations or emergencies. Also called eustress, positive stress boosts cognitive and behavioral reactions that are more helpful for your well-being rather than harmful.

Consider that burst of nerves just before a game-winning play and the boost of concentration. Or the pressing voice that gets you off the couch and the phone to study for a test tomorrow.

The type of stress with beneficial impact is acute or moderate, where the body returns to a state of rest after a short while. Chronic stress has the potential to cause grievous harm and deteriorates the mind, body, and spirit.

Potential benefits of positive stress include:

1. Stress may boost brain growth

Researchers at UC Berkeley embarked on a study of the effect of stress on rats and examined the growth of stem cells in the hippocampus part of the brain (Kirby et al., 2013). The hippocampus plays a role in stress response, learning, and memory. The study showed that stem cell growth is stimulated when rats are exposed to moderate stress for a short period (for example, immobilization for a few hours), and the cells form neurons. In addition, tests after a few weeks showed learning and memory improvement.

On the flip side, when the rats were exposed to chronic stress, such as immobilization for days at a time, stem cell growth was limited, and fewer brain cells were generated.

2. Stress may improve memory

When animals experience stress, say wandering across a predator's path and narrowly escaping death, their brain registers the place and encounter. Moderate pressure prompts the development of specialized cells, which help memorize this stressful experience. The animal is then likely to remember the event and avoid the place it happened and therefore preserve its life. The animal is also likely to be more alert to the environment and what is a potential threat or not (University of California- Berkeley, 2013).

Even where moderate stress does not necessarily endanger our lives, exposure to the stressor boosts memory alongside our focus, helping us rise to the challenge better.

On the other hand, stress may make us more forgetful, say when nervous before a test. In this case, relaxation techniques like breathwork help to return to calm. Moreover, talking yourself into changing how you view your capacity to tackle the obstacle may help convert the distress into eustress and reap the benefits of the energy and memory boost.

3. Stress may help get into the flow

Have you found yourself stressed about a looming test or deadline and suddenly felt a rush of focus? Mild stress sometimes helps the brain shut out all other tasks and concentrate on the one at hand. Surprisingly, the pressure may also stimulate the cog to turn faster, and a job that would have taken all day takes half the time.

This is why some people spend the whole night before a big test studying their heap of notes but cannot pull off the same feat in the middle of the term.

Chronic stress is the opposite and increases fatigue and difficulty concentrating on tasks. Therefore, a person dealing with prolonged stress is more likely to be overwhelmed by assignments requiring focus.

4. Stress helps keep you balanced

Stress is a normal part of life, and no one is exempt from stressful situations. We are all sometimes late for an appointment, caught in traffic, dealing with a tragedy, or stressed at work.

While chronic stress is unhealthy and requires immediate management, mild to moderate pressure keeps you rooted in your humanity. The awareness that everybody copes with one form of anxiety or another helps you understand that you are not unlucky or cursed. You are just living a normal life like anyone else.

Of course, this knowledge is not to encourage acceptance of stress and its debilitating effects without change. Instead, it ought to make you aware of the stressors in your daily life and the healthy coping mechanisms available.

5. Stress helps build resilience

In addition to stress keeping us balanced, pressure builds a thick skin. None of us is free from the adversities of life, so how does one turn the exposure from a bad experience to a helpful one?

The first time a stressful event happened may have been challenging to handle. However, facing the situation made you aware of your strengths and ability to conquer, probably improving how you handle similar cases in future.

To put it to the test, think about a stressful situation you have been in. You may have got a flat tire on your way to work. Perhaps you had a child that had to go to the hospital in the middle of the night. Think about the first time you remember something like this happening. It may have been months or a few years ago.

How did you feel that first time? What thoughts went through your mind? What did you do to resolve the issue? Write out what you remember below.

_____

_____

_____

_____

Now, think about the next time the same incident or something similar happened. Your car broke down on the way to a meeting, or another family member came down with something. How did it feel this time, given that you had been in a similar situation before? How were your reactions? Was it just as overwhelming as the first time? Did you feel more equipped to cope? Share what you remember being the same or different below.

_____

_____

_____

_____

The exposure to stress also helps us learn the different coping strategies that work in varying stressful situations. Even where the situation did not turn out as well as we would have hoped, the experience is a learning point for what worked and what did not and what we could do differently next time.

6. Stress may enhance child development

Research shows that babies born to mothers experiencing mild to moderate stress during pregnancy had higher developmental skills by age two than babies born to unstressed mothers (Dipietro et al., 2021). Further research found that people who experienced brief stress, such as separation from their mother for a short period in their early life, had better brain function and less anxiety as adults.

These findings do not mean expectant mothers should deliberately introduce stress into their pregnancy. On the contrary, extended stress in infancy and childhood is linked to negative consequences in a person's early life and adulthood.

These findings suggest that even if you find yourself in a few stressful situations, they are not necessarily devastating to the baby. With proper stress management techniques, mild stress can be a stimulant for both the parent and the child.

7. Stress may help build immunity

Small doses of stress raise the immunity level and the body's ability to fight illnesses by stimulating the production of chemicals called interleukins. This may explain why that flu catching everyone else seems to be no threat to you.

The effect of mild stress on immunity is unlike chronic stress, which eventually increases the body's vulnerability to infections and inflammations.

8. Stress may have social and emotional benefits

Going through a stressful situation such as a terminally ill family member or grief is difficult. Yet these challenging moments become manageable when we have strong social support. Stress can help deepen these bonds and the appreciation for such individuals in one's life.

Moreover, triggering events are like storms. While they are taxing to endure, they remind us of the calm, sunlit days and help us appreciate the latter seasons more. They give perspective and meaning to life, allowing us to view the motions we go through with a keener and less rigid lens.

The Causes of Stress

Everyone has different stress triggers depending on the circumstances that make up their life. However, many stressors fall into one of the categories below:

1. Work stressors

Unfavorable work conditions are a significant cause of stress across the world (Bhui et al., 2016)

Workplace triggers that could contribute to stress include:

- Too heavy workload or too much responsibility
- Long work hours

- Unclear work expectations or no say in the decision-making process
- Hazardous working conditions such as an unsafe neighborhood, risky operation, etc
- Job insecurity like threat/ risk of termination and limited opportunities for growth
- Uncomfortable situations such as giving presentations in front of colleagues
- Harassment or discrimination
- General unhappiness with the job

Sometimes, the factors causing stress at work are outside the job itself, including general health, personal life problems like relationship conflicts, and lack of emotional support while coping with job pressures.

How can you tell that you or a colleague are starting to suffer under work stress?

Behavior that may be linked to job stress include:

- Work performance takes a plunge
- Decreasing sense of initiative and creativity
- Irritability, diminished patience, and increased frustration
- Strife in personal relationships as the frustration seeps into other areas
- Isolation from colleagues

Do you deal with these or any other stressors at the workplace? Can you identify any ways you may behave due to stress at work? Share any personal observations below.

_____

_____

_____

_____

2. Financial stressors

Money is an enormous source of stress for a majority of the earth's population. Almost everything requires a financial injection- taking your kids to school, going on vacation, having a roof over your head, taking care of your health, everything.

Financial instability is stressful because it curtails the ability to meet these responsibilities, and the consequences compound the frustration, extending the symptoms and effects of stress. Poverty is a significant driver of chronic stress, which can remain an undercurrent even when the impoverished seem to have made peace with their lot.

Sometimes, we may not be aware that we are stressed about money or are acting out. These symptoms are some of what it looks like when money is a continuous stressor:

- Constant arguments with loved ones whenever the subject of money comes up
- Growing anxiety about picking up phone calls or opening the mail for fear that the callers have come to collect
- Guilt about spending money on non-essential items or spoiling yourself even when it is once in a while
- Constant worry about money, even if the current obligations are handled

Have you recently found yourself worrying about money? What are some of the things you have found yourself thinking, feeling, or doing as a result of this stress?

_____

_____

_____

_____

3. **Personal relationship stressors**

Personal relationships are life-giving in a world that can be quite lonely. Yet these same relationships can cause significant distress. Relationships with family members, intimate partners, children, colleagues, and friends can either be the sources of stress or affected by other stressors.

For example, intimate relationships often suffer under these common issues:

- Miscommunication or no communication
- Busyness, e.g. with work, limiting the interaction time
- Reduced intimacy owing to work, health challenges, etc
- Disagreement leading to conversations about divorce
- Overconsumption of drugs and alcohol.

Parenting is another ballgame which carries plenty to worry about in addition to the joys of raising children. The sources of stress for parents include:

- Financial distress due to low income or job instability
- Long work hours and limited time and energy for the kids
- Single parenting is difficult for any individual, especially without support
- Marital or relationship problems which affect kids directly or indirectly
- Raising a child with a developmental disability- this is a significant stress factor for parents (Hsiao, 2018)

4. Internal stressors

Sometimes the stressors come from within.

For example, we may experience fear and uncertainty about events we cannot control, such as epidemics, war, and terrorism. This same fear may trickle into closer events like worrying that you cannot finish a job in time, accelerating the response to that stress. Suppose your mind is constantly on all the things that are anxiety-triggering. In that case, it will readily identify and ruminate over other stressors, even though it could have been easier to handle these local challenges without the dark cloud.

Similarly, our attitude and perception greatly influence how we react to stress. Consider a salary delay when the bills are due. You could think, *'I know these bills are pressing, but I can do nothing until I get paid. I will call the landlord and ask them for more time.'*

Alternatively, you could think, *'I am in so much trouble. What if I get an eviction notice and cannot talk my way out?'*

Though the attitude with which we approach stressful events may not necessarily solve the problem, a positive outlook does help to stop magnifying the problem. Not frantic with worry, a clear head will also help think through feasible solutions, enabling more progressive problem-solving.

5. Daily life stressors

Daily life is full of small and large events that can trigger stress. Think about all the times you forgot your keys or essential documents, had a delayed flight, got late or missed an appointment, and so forth.

While these events are random and mostly the prompts for short-term stress, the effects can extend if the frustration goes unmanaged for too long. Being aware of the little slip-ups and how to avoid them can help. For example, if you forget your keys a few times, nurture the habit of placing them close to the door at an obvious, unmissable spot. If you tend to get late to appointments, work on leaving the house or office earlier so that any inconveniences will not be too damaging.

6. Change

Significant life changes, even positive ones, can be stressful. Change implies a shift from one state of being and routine to another, and the adjustment is not always automatic and effortless.

Positive changes that can bring about stress include getting married, a job promotion, having a baby, etc.

Unsettling changes likely to cause unrest include the death of a loved one, divorce, a huge financial setback, getting fired, etc.

Techniques for Stress Management

Though stressful events hit us occasionally, the effects of this trigger often depend on how we perceive the situation. From a cognitive behavioral perspective, we are often stressed by how we feel about a stressor. And we experience those feelings because of how we think about a situation.

Let us consider Chris and Jenna, both stuck in traffic on their way home one rainy evening.

Chris is angry at how slow the drivers in front of him are inching forward. He keeps honking every few minutes and yelling at everyone and no one.

His thought process and subsequent emotions and behavior may be something like this:

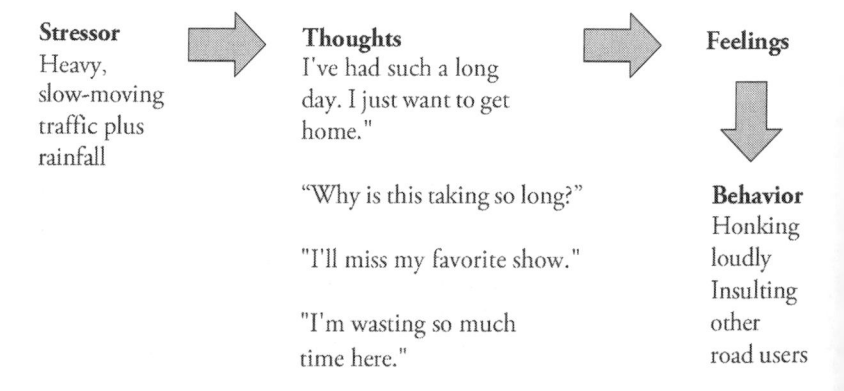

Stressor	Thoughts	Feelings
Heavy, slow-moving traffic plus rainfall	"I've had such a long day. I just want to get home."	
	"Why is this taking so long?"	**Behavior**
	"I'll miss my favorite show."	Honking loudly
	"I'm wasting so much time here."	Insulting other road users

On the other hand, Jenna rolls up her window and puts on her favorite playlist. She breathes in and out calmly while planning her next day.

Her cognitive behavioral process may be something like this:

Stressor
Heavy, slow-moving traffic plus rainfall

→

Thoughts
I've had such a long day. This is a perfect time to unwind."

"I haven't listened to my music without needing to accommodate others in a while."

"I might be late getting home, but I'll be relaxed."

→

Feelings
Ease, calm, blissful

↓

Behavior
Plays favorite playlist

Does breathing techniques

Plans for tomorrow

As the illustrations above indicate, we can manage stress by managing our approach to each situation. As such, the techniques below are some of the means to manage stress and improve our health and well-being effectively.

1. Identify the current strategies to manage stress

As we have seen in the previous chapters, awareness is the first step towards progress. How do you deal with the unpleasant feelings that arise out of stressful conditions? Understanding how you react to situations can help you determine if there are gaps in how you do things now and how to handle stress better moving forward.

Consider the questions below and answer them honestly. If unsure, ask a trusted friend or family member for their observations and compare them with how you view yourself.

Activity Box:

The activity below is meant to help visualize how you are presently dealing with stress triggers. The questions evaluate how you react to the feelings associated with stress and how you behave when stressed.

These questions are not comprehensive- they are mostly a guide to help assess some of the positive and negative responses you may have to stress.

Answer 'yes' or 'no' to each question.

1. Do you quash or dismiss upsetting feelings?

2. Do you allow recurring thoughts that increase the upsetting feelings?

3. Do you distract yourself from stressful situations by watching TV, going on social media, drinking, eating, etc?

4. Do you avoid or run away from stressful situations?

5. Do you talk yourself through the feelings of worry, anxiety, fear, or other stress-related emotions?

6. Do you talk out when stressed and seek help, e.g. from a therapist, friends, etc?

7. Do you substitute bad thoughts with good ones?

8. Do you put off important tasks when experiencing upsetting feelings?

9. Do you engage in pleasant activities like hobbies when experiencing extended feelings of stress?

10. Do you lash out at the people around you when in a stressful situation?

Share any thoughts and emotions that sprung up while completing this exercise in the space below.

_____

_____

_____

_____

_____

Review the answers above and think about the actions that bring short-term relief and those that offer long-term relief.

Short-term, in this case, could mean a few hours or days before the discomforting feelings return. Long-term could mean weeks, months, or even years. Fill in the short-term and the long-term relief strategies in the fields below.

The entries may include other things that occurred to you in the course of the exercise not included in the questions above:

Short-term Relief Responses	Long-term Relief Responses

Finally, consider these strategies and how they make you feel. Do they help soothe the unsettling feelings? Do they help resolve the cause of stress, or how you react to it? Do you feel progressively able to cope with each stressful event as it occurs? Is there anything missing?

Share your thoughts below:

_____

_____

_____

_____

2. Change the view towards stressful situations

In the recent past, CBT has taken a more acceptance-oriented route. Techniques such as the Acceptance and Commitment Therapy (ACT) have shown remarkable value for people learning to manage stress and consequent disorders like depression and anxiety (Twohig & Levin, 2017).

These techniques aim to accept what you are already experiencing rather than struggle to reduce stress and anxiety. Then, you get to choose how you would like your life to go moving forward and finally take actionable steps towards the envisioned goals.

Radical acceptance is often integrated into Dialectical Behavioral Therapy (DBT), a modification of CBT that focuses on teaching patients to live in the present and learn strategies to manage emotions, cope with stress, and improve social relationships.

Acceptance begins by understanding that you cannot control every aspect of every experience. For example, you cannot control how people respond or react to your behavior. You can, however, accept the parts beyond your control and focus instead on your actions.

ACTIVITY I

Reaction vs Response

Consider an event that was quite stressful for you. It could be personal life or work-related. It could be in the recent past or a long while ago (if you remember the details). Bring as many details to mind while answering the questions below:

a. What was the pain point?

What happened before the stressful event? How did it happen? Who was there when it happened? How did you feel about the occurrence of the event?

_____

_____

_____

_____

_____

b. What role did your actions play in the situation?

How did you act or react to the stressful event? What did you say or do? How did your actions make you feel?

_____

_____

_____

_____

_____

c. What role did other people's behavior play?

What did the people around you do to contribute to the stressful event? How did their actions influence the situation?

_____
_____
_____
_____
_____
_____
_____

d. What was your level of control?

What was within your control in the situation? What could you not control?

_____
_____
_____
_____
_____
_____
_____

e. What was the impact of your behavior?

How did the people around you behave as a result of your actions regarding the stressful event? What did they say or do after your behavior?

_____

_____

_____

_____

_____

f. What could you do next time to minimize the painful experience?

A reaction is quick and without thought, and emotions guide the behavior. A response, on the other hand, is more deliberate, thought-out, and rational. While we cannot control all the elements around a stressful situation, we can learn to respond rather than react.

What could you have done in this situation to minimize the emotional reaction? How could you behave to calmly address the circumstance at hand and reduce the distressing emotions you experienced? What could you do differently next time?

_____

_____

ACTIVITY II

Setting Radical Goals

Radical acceptance gets easier with practice. It is like exercising a muscle. The more we do it, the more we can do it.

Consider what you might like to accept moving forward radically. Remember, radical acceptance means letting go of the need to control the situation and instead managing how you respond to it. The more you catch your emotional reactions, the more you take steps to respond calmly.

a. What small stressful things would you like to accept radically? The list can be longer, but 3-5 small radical goals are sufficient.

Illustration: Encountering a rude waitperson at a random coffee shop

b. What medium stressful things would you like to accept radically? The list can be longer, but 3-5 medium radical goals are sufficient.

   Illustration: Experiencing a power cut in the middle of studying for an exam.

   _____
   _____
   _____
   _____
   _____

c. What significant stressful things would you like to accept radically? The list can be longer, but 3-5 meaningful radical goals are sufficient.

   Illustration: losing a job or significant client

   _____
   _____
   _____
   _____
   _____

At the end of this workbook, we shall review these goals and your progress towards radical acceptance.

3. Maintaining calmness

A sense of calmness helps to manage stress and other disorders like anxiety. Breathwork, meditation, and grounding techniques help bring the mind back to a place of peace. When we are calm in mind, the rest of the body relaxes and the symptoms of stress, such as labored breathing, ease.

4. Elevate positive emotions

Emotions like joy and gratitude are easy to build up when things are good. Yet it is when things are particularly bleak that they are more impactful. Feeling grateful for what you have in the middle of a storm helps create the mindset that it's not all bad. Remembering hope in a desperate situation can keep you from slipping into destructive habits to cope.

So, keeping a stock of positive emotions is a powerful tool to help maintain calm before and during stressful events. Increasing the attitude of positivity has long-term benefits, improving how you view yourself over time and building confidence and reassurance that you can handle everything life throws at you.

ACTIVITY I

Building the Emotions Wallet

In the fields below, make notes for positive emotions. There is a vast array of emotions to choose from, and we shall focus on joy, hope, gratitude, pride, peace, and inspiration. Use as many resources that come to mind, including memories, songs, images, and videos.

a. Joy

When have you felt that everything was its best? When have you felt complete joy? What things bring out a genuine smile?

_____
_____
_____
_____
_____

b. Hope

When have you felt hopeful? When did you believe something good would happen even if you feared the worst? What is it like to be filled with hope? When have you tried to design a better tomorrow for yourself?

_____
_____
_____
_____
_____
_____

c. Gratitude

What are you grateful for? When have you felt most grateful? When were you thankful for something or someone, even when things weren't perfect?

_____

_____

_____

_____

_____

_____

d. Pride

When have you felt proud of yourself for doing something? What achievements, big or small, have you made up to this point? What would you give yourself a medal for?

_____

_____

_____

_____

_____

_____

e. Peace

When do you feel most at peace? What activities or motions put you in a state of relaxation? When did you feel utter peace and calm?

_____

_____

_____

_____

_____

f. Inspiration

When were you most motivated to do your best? When were you in the pursuit of excellence? What is it like to feel inspired to be your best self?

_____

_____

_____

_____

_____

The Role of Sustainable Self-care

Regarding mental health and overall well-being, progress is only possible with self-care- For example, stress multiplies when inadequately rested and underfed. Rolling fatigue increases the difficulty concentrating on tasks and promotes spill-over effects like procrastination, creating an endless, deteriorative cycle.

Remember the activity in chapter two that looked at the facets of your life? Think through the questions below and assess how well you care for yourself. Review the answers in the previous chapter to compare your thoughts then and now.

1. Are you eating a balanced diet?
   Are you undereating, overeating, or eating just right?
   What does your plate look like?

_____

_____

_____

_____

2. Are you getting enough sleep?
   Do you wake up feeling rested?
   How many hours of sleep are you getting every night?

_____

_____

_____

_____

3. Are you putting in any physical activity? Do you get regular exercise?

_____
_____
_____
_____

4. Do you spend time with the people you love? Do you prioritize and make time for the people in your life?

_____
_____
_____
_____
_____

5. Are you working on things you are passionate about? Do you enjoy the way you spend your days?

_____
_____
_____
_____
_____

6. Do you spend time by yourself?
   Do you like your own company and do fun things with your lonesome?

   _____

   _____

   _____

   _____

If there are *no*'s or vague answers to the questions above, review each and evaluate how you might improve them for better overall health. For example, if you do not get adequate sleep, you could check your routine and work in early bedtimes.

This chapter has looked at the various stressors we encounter throughout our lives. We considered the types of stress, their effects, and the benefits of short-term, positive pressure. Finally, we looked at CBT techniques to help manage chronic stress. Stress management is vital when managing other disorders like anxiety and depression. Challenging the negative thoughts that spur stress makes it easier to walk through anxiety and panic attacks. It helps relieve the overwhelmed mind, making it easier to get past the depressive mood and out of bed. Life will always throw stressors. We must not be avoiders but effective managers.

Winding Up

The journey of a thousand miles begins with a single step. You took that step when you opened this workbook and have made enormous strides to get to this checkpoint. Take a moment to breathe. Inhale. Exhale. Again. Reflect on the adventure.

There have been numerous activities across this workbook. In the earlier chapters, we laid out your life map in the various facets that come together to form you. We worked towards the goals you would like to accomplish with the help of this resource and the role of CBT in effecting change.

In the latter parts of the book, we zeroed in on anxiety, depression, and stress, interlinked disorders that diminish our overall productivity and well-being. We considered the tools to help manage these conditions, focusing on changing the negative thoughts and behavior that accelerate internal suffering.

We repeatedly returned to the cognitive-behavioral cycle, looking at the interconnectedness of thoughts, emotions, and behavior.

Thoughts

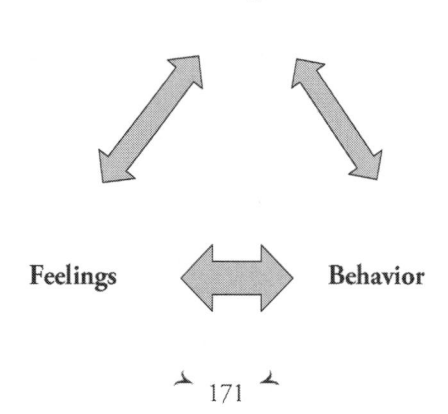

Feelings ⟷ **Behavior**

Consider these questions below.

What parts went well? What activities and chapters felt like a win? Share your reflections below.

_____

_____

_____

_____

What parts proved challenging? What activities were you uninspired to work through? Note the recollections below.

_____

_____

_____

_____

A significant portion of this workbook has required attention to what your mind says. Listening to our mind and actually hearing what it says can be difficult, especially with automatic thoughts that flit by so quickly. Yet a successful CBT program requires you to keep trying to be observant.

What was your experience, consciously and intentionally seeing and hearing your mind?

Was this a useful method? Are there patterns you realized as a result of the continuous monitoring?

_____
_____
_____
_____

Did any thoughts strike you as needing more inspection? Perhaps thoughts that you had not noticed before but which had been impacting your mood or behavior?

_____
_____
_____
_____

Did you have challenges observing your mind? Are there times the process felt obscure, unhelpful, or undoable?

_____
_____
_____
_____

How do you feel about the whole experience? How do you feel about yourself, the people around you, and the world?

_____

_____

_____

_____

Now, revisit the goals you had at the beginning of this program. What is the progress? Are there goals that are already accomplished? Are there goals that are moving steadily? Are there goals that are lagging? Share your evaluation below.

_____

_____

_____

_____

When we set goals, we like to believe that we will achieve them in the desired timeline. In reality, the work takes longer as we discover new elements to consider and work on. The key to pushing forward is focusing on progress rather than perfection. Therefore, be patient if there are unaccomplished goals and some lag.

Instead, review the work you have put into each goal and identify the challenges. Are there events that happened while working through this workbook that made it difficult to stay consistent? Are there things you discovered about yourself that need more time and reflection?

_____

_____

_____

_____

What about the goals that are going well? What factors have helped keep the momentum? Remember that all of these could be internal and external variables.

_____

_____

_____

_____

Are there new goals that came to mind during the work? Would you like to add them to the list of things you want to accomplish in the near future? Write them down below, if any.

Don't sweat it if there are none.

_____

_____

_____

_____

The Next Page

As we have seen extensively, consistency is the key to progress. Now that the workbook is over, the ball is on your court. How do you keep dribbling and making those hoops?

- → Stay vigilant
  Continue to observe the comings and goings of your thoughts. Mindfulness and awareness are a lifestyle, not a single event.

- → Stay aware of your triggers so your motions do not catch you off-guard. When the triggers occur, remind yourself that you are in control, and your body can relax and allow you to handle the situation.

- → Acknowledge that some days will be difficult. As Epictetus remarked, no great thing is created suddenly. Focus on making progress, even when that feels like a wiggle or a crawl.

- → On this note, make a list of reminders that motivate you to stay on course. These reminders could be what you are fighting for, the new belief you have or want to have about yourself, or anything close to the heart that is inspiring.

My list of reminders:

1.

2.

3.

4.

5.

→ To add to these reminders, go back to the list of strengths often, adding new qualities as you learn yourself anew. You could note them again below, praising yourself for each one.

_____

_____

_____

_____

Similarly, review your emotions wallet often. Returning to the things that make you joyful, hopeful, motivated, and grateful will cushion the heart on the bleak days.

→ If you did not find the workbook particularly helpful or could use further assistance, consult a professional.

A good therapist is trained to walk through every hurdle with you and keep you on course. Your progress is what matters the most. Do not be afraid to ask for help when you need it.

One Last Note

Writing this book has been life-changing. Each activity has allowed me to see my life and experiences through a fresh lens, and I am honored to have traveled this road with you.

There is so much to uncover about our minds and mental health that this workbook barely scratches the surface. So the work continues, and gloriously so!

Take a moment to reflect on the general experience. Was this workbook helpful? Are there questions you would like answered in subsequent titles and editions? Please leave a review on Amazon, highlighting the parts you enjoyed and would like to plough through in the subsequent reads.

And now, my friend, as Elizabeth Gilbert says towards the end of Eat, Pray, Love, "attraversiamo". Let us cross over (Gilbert, 2007). I am excited about what your new life holds.

Thank You

Thank you so much for purchasing my book.

There were dozens of options, but you took a chance on this book.

Thank you for taking this journey with me and making it all the way to the end.

Before you go, allow me to ask for a tiny favor. Would you please consider posting a review on the platform? It only takes 5 seconds.

Posting a review is the best and easiest way to support the work of independent authors like me.

Your feedback will help me keep writing and sharing the books and resources to propel you towards your desired results.

Hearing from you would mean the world.

https://www.amazon.com/review/create-review

References

Albert Camus Quotes - Citation. (n.d.). BrainyQuote. Retrieved April 1, 2023, from https://www.brainyquote.com/citation/quotes/albert_camus_134051

Arends, I. (2015). Fit Mind, Fit Job. *OECD eBooks*. https://doi.org/10.1787/9789264228283-en

Aristotle Quote: "Knowing yourself is the beginning of all wisdom." (n.d.). Quote Fancy. Retrieved April 1, 2023, from https://quotefancy.com/quote/245/Aristotle-Knowing-yourself-is-the-beginning-of-all-wisdom

Beck, A. T., Rush, A. J., Shaw, B. F., & Emery, G. (1979). *Cognitive Therapy of Depression*. Guilford Press.

Bhui, K., Dinos, S., Galant-Miecznikowska, M., De Jongh, B., & Stansfeld, S. (2016). Perceptions of work stress causes and effective interventions in employees working in public, private and non-governmental organisations: a qualitative study. *BJPsych Bulletin, 40*(6), 318–325. https://doi.org/10.1192/pb.bp.115.050823

Big Mouth. (2017). Danger Goldberg Productions, Good at Bizness, Inc., Fathouse Industries. https://www.netflix.com/ke/title/80117038

Chocano, C. (2021, September). The Return of Selena. *Elle*. Retrieved April 1, 2023, from https://www.elle.com/culture/celebrities/a37319287/selena-gomez-interview-2021/#

Coelho, P. (2006). *Veronika Decides to Die: A Novel of Redemption*. Harper Collins.

D'Amico, D., Libro, G., Prudenzano, M. P., Peccarisi, C., Guazzelli, M., Relja, G., Puca, F., Genco, S., Maggioni, F., Nappi, G., Verri, A., Cerbo, R., & Bussone, G. (2000). Stress and chronic headache. *Journal of Headache and Pain*, *1*(S1), S49–S52. https://doi.org/10.1007/s101940070026

David, D., Cristea, I. A., & Hofmann, S. G. (2018). Why Cognitive Behavioral Therapy Is the Current Gold Standard of Psychotherapy. *Frontiers in Psychiatry*, *9*. https://doi.org/10.3389/fpsyt.2018.00004

David, D., Lynn, S. J., & Ellis, A. (2009). *Rational and Irrational Beliefs: Research, Theory, and Clinical Practice*. Oxford University Press.

Descartes, R. (2008). *A Discourse on the Method: Of Correctly Conducting One's Reason and Seeking Truth in the Sciences* (I. Maclean, Trans.). Oxford University Press.

Dipietro, J. A., Novak, M. F., Costigan, K. A., Atella, L. D., & Reusing, S. P. (2021, July 7). Mild Maternal Stress May Actually Help Children Mature. *Johns Hopkins Bloomberg School of Public Health*. Retrieved April 1, 2023, from https://publichealth.jhu.edu/2006/dipietro-stress

Dome, P., Rihmer, Z., & Gonda, X. (2019). Suicide Risk in Bipolar Disorder: A Brief Review. *Medicina-lithuania*, *55*(8), 403. https://doi.org/10.3390/medicina55080403

Dr. Pizzazz. (2021, September 13). *Grim Adventures - Mandy & Gollum [HD]* [Video]. YouTube. https://www.youtube.com/watch?v=VmmVz4eTlzQ

Ecclesiastes 9:11. (n.d.). Bible Gateway. https://www.biblegateway.com/verse/en/Ecclesiastes%209:11

Epictetus. (1865). *The Works of Epictetus: Consisting of His Discourses, in Four Books, the Enchiridion, and Fragments.*

Fancourt, D., Steptoe, A., & Bu, F. (2021). Trajectories of anxiety and depressive symptoms during enforced isolation due to COVID-19 in England: a longitudinal observational study. *The Lancet Psychiatry, 8*(2), 141–149. https://doi.org/10.1016/s2215-0366(20)30482-x

Freud, S. (1955). *The Standard Edition of the Complete Psychological Works of Sigmund Freud* (Vol. 2). Hogarth Press.

Gilbert, E. (2007). *Eat, Pray, Love: One Woman's Search for Everything.* A&C Black.

Hofmann, S. G., Asnaani, A., Vonk, I. J. J., Sawyer, A. T., & Fang, A. (2012). The Efficacy of Cognitive Behavioral Therapy: A Review of Meta-analyses. *Cognitive Therapy and Research, 36*(5), 427–440. https://doi.org/10.1007/s10608-012-9476-1

Hsiao, Y. (2018). Parental Stress in Families of Children With Disabilities. *Intervention in School and Clinic, 53*(4), 201–205. https://doi.org/10.1177/1053451217712956

The 'Iceberg Metaphor'-Freud's vision of the mind [54]- Scientific Diagram. (n.d.). ResearchGate. Retrieved April 1, 2023, from https://www.researchgate.net/figure/The-Iceberg-Metaphor-Freuds-vision-of-the-mind-54_fig2_282489228/

https://doi.org/10.59158/001c.71013

Kirby, E. D., Muroy, S. E., Sun, W. G., Covarrubias, D., Leong, M. J., Barchas, L. A., & Kaufer, D. (2013). Acute stress enhances adult rat hippocampal neurogenesis and activation of newborn neurons via secreted astrocytic FGF2. *eLife*, *2*. https://doi.org/10.7554/elife.00362

Locke, J. (1690). An Essay concerning Human Understanding. *Oxford University Press eBooks*, 1. https://doi.org/10.1093/oseo/instance.00018020

Marcus Aurelius Quotes. (n.d.). BrainyQuote. Retrieved April 1, 2023, from https://www.brainyquote.com/quotes/marcus_aurelius_121534

Matthew 5:45. (n.d.). Bible Hub. Retrieved April 1, 2023, from https://www.biblehub.com/matthew/5-45.htm

Mondragon, B. C. (n.d.). *Emily Elizabeth Dickinson - Neurotic Poets*. Neurotic Poets. Retrieved April 11, 2023, from https://neuroticpoets.com/dickinson

Nakao, M., Shirotsuki, K., & Sugaya, N. (2021a). Cognitive–behavioral therapy for management of mental health and stress-related disorders: Recent advances in techniques and technologies. *Biopsychosocial Medicine*. https://doi.org/10.1186/s13030-021-00219-w

Nakao, M., Shirotsuki, K., & Sugaya, N. (2021b). Cognitive–behavioral therapy for management of mental health and stress-related disorders: Recent advances in techniques and technologies. *Biopsychosocial Medicine*, *15*(1). https://doi.org/10.1186/ s13030-021-00219-w

Riebe, G., Fan, M., Unützer, J., & Vannoy, S. D. (2012). Activity scheduling as a core component of effective care management for late-life depression. *International Journal of Geriatric Psychiatry, 27*(12), 1298–1304. https://doi.org/10.1002/gps.3784

Rowling, J. K. (2000). The Pensieve. In *Harry Potter and the Goblet of Fire* (British Children's Edition, pp. 371–386). Bloomsbury.

Rowling, J. K. (2005). The House of Gaunt. In *Harry Potter and the Half Blood Prince* (British Children's Edition, pp. 130–144). Bloomsbury.

Salazar, F. (Ed.). (2018). *Big Mouth| The Department of Puberty* (season 2, episode 10). Danger Goldberg Productions, Good at Bizness, Inc., Fathouse Industries. Retrieved April 1, 2023, from https://www.netflix.com/ke/title/80117038

Selye, H. (1956). *The Stress of Life*.

Shakespeare, W. (2017). *The Complete Works of William Shakespeare| The Merchant of Venice*. Delphi Classics. (Original work published 1598)

Srivastava, R., Jain, N., & Singhal, A. K. (2005). Influence of alternate nostril breathing on cardiorespiratory and autonomic functions in healthy young adults. *Indian Journal of Physiology and Pharmacology, 49*(4), 475–483.

Szabo, A., & Hopkinson, K. L. (2007). Negative psychological effects of watching the news in the television: Relaxation or another intervention may be needed to buffer them! *International Journal of Behavioral Medicine, 14*(2), 57–62. https://doi.org/10.1007/bf03004169

Tolle, E. (2005). *A New Earth: Awakening to Your Life's Purpose.* Christian Large Print.

Tseng, J., & Poppenk, J. (2020). Brain meta-state transitions demarcate thoughts across task contexts exposing the mental noise of trait neuroticism. *Nature Communications, 11*(1). https://doi.org/10.1038/s41467-020-17255-9

Twohig, M. P., & Levin, M. (2017). Acceptance and Commitment Therapy as a Treatment for Anxiety and Depression. *Psychiatric Clinics of North America, 40*(4), 751–770. https://doi.org/10.1016/j.psc.2017.08.009

Tyler, A. (2022, September). What Condition Did Floki Have In Vikings? *ScreenRant.* https://www.msn.com/en-us/tv/recaps/what-condition-did-floki-have-in-vikings/ar-AA11xflc

University of California- Berkeley. (2013, April 13). *Acute stress primes brain for better cognitive and mental performance.* ScienceDaily. https://www.sciencedaily.com/releases/2013/04/130416204546.htm

Vanzant, I. (2001). *Faith in the Valley: Lessons for Women on the Journey to Peace.* Simon and Schuster.

William James Quote: "The greatest weapon against stress is our ability to choose one thought over another." (n.d.). Quote Fancy. Retrieved April 1, 2023, from https://quotefancy.com/quote/28852/William-James-The-greatest-weapon-against-stress-is-our-ability-to-choose-one-thought

World Health Organization: WHO. (2023, March 31). Depressive disorder (depression). *www.who.int.* https://www.who.int/news-room/fact-sheets/detail/depression

Printed in Great Britain
by Amazon